The Cotswolds

40 Town and Country Walks

D1462828

In memory of ADN (1931-1999), ADP (1937-2003) and MDN (1960-2007)

published by
pocket mountains ltd
Holm Street, Moffat
Dumfries and Galloway
DG10 9EB

ISBN: 978-1-9070251-9-8

A catalogue record for this book is available from the British Library

Contains Ordnance Survey data © Crown copyright and database right 2014, supported by out of copyright mapping from 1945-1961

Printed in Poland

Introduction

A gentle upland, cut by river valleys (some shallow, some narrow), rolling in waves to its edge, then falling away into flat cropland; wooded, but not especially so; settled and inhabited, but not especially so. There are, it has to be said, more dramatic landscapes in England – mountains, lakes, white cliffs, even the odd gorge. Why is it, then, that the Cotswolds, that gentle upland bridging the West Country with the Midlands, is so prized?

It is certainly beautiful, one easy-on-the-eye view reaching to another; unspoilt too, or at least largely unchallenged by obvious modernity. But for all that, the appeal of the Cotswolds burrows somewhat deeper than mere aesthetic appreciation: here we find, perhaps more clearly than anywhere else, something deeply reassuring – a sense of harmony. It is a harmony sprung from a centuries-long union between the land and those who have lived, worked and built upon it. A patchwork legacy, traced from prehistory through the Romans, the Tudors, the Jacobeans and, in particular, the Georgians – paths worn down from generations of feet, land carefully husbanded, and a built environment hewn from the material upon which it stands. Consider the way a medieval church nestles within a honey stone village, ringed by pastures, hedgerow-lined lanes and shaded copses, while behind rises a low-slung ridge – the Cotswolds is the exemplar of rural England, the image that forms in the mind of the overseas visitor when asked to conjure the English landscape, the near-perfect fusion of landscape and history.

That the Cotswolds have survived as they have in the south of this crowded island is some sort of minor miracle. Caught in a triangle of motorways and ringed by large and medium-sized cities of industrial heritage (though only 160,000 people live within the designated Area of Outstanding Natural Beauty, there are two million within a 20-minute drive), the Cotswolds rise as an island of rusticity, largely spared the march of the Industrial Revolution and the development that followed. Perhaps it was the lack of coal, the prosperity of the wool trade, the preservation instincts of the local gentry and landowners, but slowly and unequivocally the pace of life in the Cotswolds was left behind and, as other places changed, the agrarian air of the Cotswolds stayed largely the same. In certain places, it is quite easy to believe the scene unchanged for hundreds of years. With that beauty, harmony and patina of history, the Cotswolds became a comforting refuge, a route back to the past (there are more listed buildings, for instance, within the boundary of the Cotswold District Council then in any other district in England). Once it was William Morris and other prominent members of the Arts & Crafts Movement fleeing the capital and settling here – nostalgic, even then, for a simpler age.

Today it is more likely a city banker relocating his family or the ex-rock star settling down to making organic cheese. Going back to nature in the Cotswolds has always been a well-to-do business.

All is not still here, however. Behind the sleepy villages and stately manor houses there is a vibrant agricultural mix – from barley and wheat to fruit farms, riverside meadows and open grazing – that is perhaps second only to tourism in the area's economic make-up. Busy market towns such as Stroud, Cirencester and Chipping Norton ('Chipping' deriving from the Old English for 'market') hum to the beat of commerce and of getting things done. Then, at the periphery, there are

Oxford and Bath, historic cities as fine as any England can offer.

This is a place that invites slow travel – poking around, dawdling, lingering, reflecting. There is no better way to do that, of course, than on foot. Indeed, it would be hard to imagine a more walking-friendly environment – it never demands much in the way of exertion and is always ready with a reward. It is one of the curiosities of the Cotswolds that off-the-beaten track is often much to be preferred to on-the-beaten track. Step away from the crowds and there are a thousand delightful places to discover – dots on the map (often unnamed), wildflower meadows or stands of aged beech trees. Of course, there are some places you should go to no matter how many other people have the same idea – Broadway Tower, for one, Castle

Combe for another – and out of season or at the margins of the day they live up to their billing.

About this guide

There is no particular rule as to what constitutes the Cotswolds. The most formal definition is the boundary of the Cotswolds Area of Outstanding Natural Beauty (AONB) – at 790 sq miles the largest protected landscape in England after the Lake District National Park. Everyone – administrators included – agree that eastern Gloucestershire, western Oxfordshire and a parcel of Worcestershire fall within the Cotswolds. Beyond that there is debate. The approach taken here is inspired more by history, interest and atmosphere than by lines on maps – so, yes, unlikely as it may sound, in these pages the cities of Bath and Oxford and bits of Wiltshire and Warwickshire qualify as 'the Cotswolds'.

The ground covered rises from easy valley strolls to invigorating climbs up the escarpment. None of the walks are longer than, at most, a few hours. Each route sets out the relevant Ordnance Survey (OS) 1:25,000 map (which you should consult) and an indication of the time it will take. This is intended as a rough guide to assist with planning your day, and does not allow for any of the stops you may have in mind (and there should be lots). Outside of the city walks the route map is only to be taken as a general guide.

Getting around

Like most of rural England the provision of public transport in the Cotswolds is patchy. Some places – towns, usually – are relatively easy to get to, some are served infrequently and some not at all. There is no escaping the way in which a car opens up the Cotswolds for practical exploration.

When committed to the car please exercise caution and consideration: ideally use a recognised car park (the start point often steers you in that direction anyway); if this is not an option, a small, defined parking area should be. In the rare cases where it is not, be wary of blocking gateways, lanes and passing places.

Farms and livestock

Remember the farmers. Use stiles and gates where they exist and leave them as you find them. Get to grips with the Countryside Code. Keep dogs under control, ideally on a lead, especially when close to livestock and farms. Never come between a cow and her calf – with or without a dog – and in general it is wise to give cattle a wide berth, even if that means temporarily diverting from the line of the path. Sheep dot the uplands – during lambing time farmers are particularly and understandably sensitive. Remember this is a working landscape – a little respect goes a long way. All this helps to sustain a good relationship between visitors and locals.

Cotswolds' southern terminus, citadel of golden stone, World Heritage Site, exemplar of classical elegance. History, quite literally, can be touched here, in an enduring architectural legacy that is remarkable in both its consistency and preservation. And that, perhaps, is the common thread that draws together this fine city, the honeypot villages and the splendid houses at Dyrham, Horton Court and Woodchester – a sense of undisturbed history, of a human legacy and a natural environment finding an agreeable understanding.

The southern fringe of the Cotswolds, marooned by the roaring M4, is just that, a fringe – a little straggly and ill-defined at its edges, uncertain whether it really is the Cotswolds or not. If that sounds like an invitation to immediately head north, wait, for in this attractive but slightly unremarkable landscape there are places of intense beauty and historical interest. Take Castle Combe and Lacock: hardly undiscovered – on a busy day they move to the slow jostle of the tourist beat – but they remain two of England's most photogenic villages. Then there is Bath, the

Moving north, beyond the motorway and its reminder of rushing modernity, to the Cotswold Escarpment and its western edge, the angles within the landscape become more acute, the gradients steepen, villages tuck down into the folds and the tops open to the wind. Here, it is not just the easy beauty that invites you to explore, but the promise of vivid connections to the past – from a memorial to a Tudor martyr to a prehistoric hillfort and the crumbling remains of a Georgian canal, the motorway of its day.

Summer sky in the Cotswolds ▶

The South

A stroll around Lacock

Distance 3km **Time** 1 hour
Terrain meadows, fields and paving
Map OS Explorer 155 **Access** bus (234)
from Chippenham

There's a long affinity between Lacock
and photography. The negative was
invented here, countless period dramas
have been filmed here and today cameras
click around every corner. But then Lacock
is ridiculously photogenic, albeit in a
casual, lived-in sort of way, softened by
the patina of history and the soothing
familiarity of heritage.

Start from the large National Trust car
park just to the south of the village. From
the exit, cross the road, turn right, go over
a second road and head away from the
village along the pavement. Hop onto the
raised walkway as you draw near to the

snaking humpback bridge over the River
Avon (with a fine view back and to the left
across the meadows to Lacock Abbey).
Cross the first hump and then bear left by
the fingerpost into the riverside meadow.
Pick up the obvious path, forking right at
the boggy hollow in the middle to end up
close to the far right corner of the field.
Cross a small bridge over a stream and
then a stile before bearing left with the
left-hand field edge to pass through an
arch in the hedgerow. Stick with the path
as it cuts across the next field, passing
through the gate at the end to reach the
bank of the meandering river.

The route joins the water only briefly,
following it into another field before
breaking away in a rightwards diagonal as
it curves left, soon enough meeting the
road by a stone bridge. Cross the bridge
and turn left at the junction with its pair of
thatched cottages and fine Victorian
postbox. At the bend, continue ahead on a
lane between cottages and onto a metalled
path slicing up a marginal slope.

Back at the edge of the village, turn down

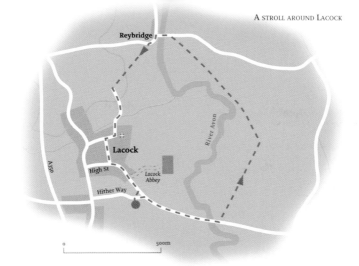

Reybridge

Lacock

High St

A350

Hither Way

Lacock Abbey

River Avon

0   500m

the road to soon reach a delightful ford at Bide Brook, bypassed by an elevated stone path and tiny double-arched bridge. Continue up to the junction.

Lacock is ideal gentle strolling territory, apparently unchanged for at least 200 years, so while the architectural styles – from Tudor to Georgian and from stone to brick – are as uneven as the rooflines, it is all strikingly harmonious.

The handsome cruciform St Cyriac's Church to the left is worth a look; otherwise bear right along Church Street and then left by the Carpenter's Arms along East Street, with the glorious restored Tithe Barn at the end on the left. By turning right at the T-junction, the High Street may be explored, though the route itself bears left towards the entrance to the abbey, found 100m on.

Free to National Trust members (otherwise paid entry), the complex offers the Fox Talbot photography museum, some manicured grounds with specimen planting, and the abbey itself, a medieval nunnery converted into a family home in the 16th century, with subsequent Gothic Revival extensions and remodelling. At the heart of it are the fascinating medieval cloisters, seen in the first two Harry Potter films. More significantly, the abbey was home to William Henry Fox Talbot, the pioneer of the negative/positive photographic process –the first known photographic negative is a view of the oriel window on the south wall of the abbey. It is a fascinating place.

To return to the car park, bear left (or continue) along the road and swing right on a path cutting through a copse.

◀ Lacock Abbey

Bath history chronicles

Distance 3km Time 1 hour 15
Terrain paved all the way
Map OS Explorer 155 Access mainline rail
and buses from all directions

A World Heritage site of breathtaking
beauty, there is no better city in England
to explore on foot than Bath.

Set out from the fountain in the middle
of Laura Place. Turn down Argyle St and
cross Pulteney Bridge, designed by Robert
Adam and completed in 1773. A Bath icon,
albeit with a Venetian air, it is apparently
one of only three bridges in the world to be
lined on both sides by shops. Continue
along Bridge St to its end and bear right,
taking the second left onto New Bond St.
Curve around to the elegant sweep of
Milsom St and amble uphill to the
T–junction at George St. Go over the
pedestrian crossing just to the right
and continue straight up cobbled
Bartlett St, remaining upwards
on the ramp to Alfred St.

Swing left to the phonebox at the end and
then right to the courtyard of the
Assembly Rooms, one of the city's finest
buildings and a hub of fashionable
Georgian society.

Bear left along Bennett St, arriving
almost immediately at The Circus, a ring of
beautifully proportioned and detailed
terraces. In April 1942, Bath was hit in a so-
called Baedeker Raid (the targets chosen
from the travel guide); one bomb landed
on The Circus destroying several houses,
though these were subsequently rebuilt.
Make the round and leave west along
Brock St to reach the enduring icon of the
city, the Royal Crescent. Much more
imposing than the Circus, the perfectly
sustained façade hides the secret that
every house behind is different –
purchasers would secure a length of
frontage, then commission their own
architect to build the actual house.

Follow the crescent to its end and then
turn down the road by the Marlborough
Buildings. After 100m, swing left onto a
path, the Gravel Walk, cutting along the
foot of the field. Continue past the rear
gardens of the houses lining the south

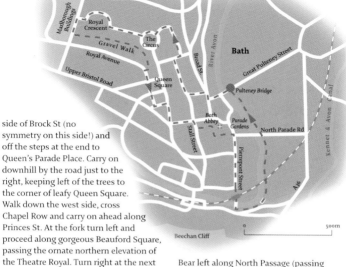

side of Brock St (no symmetry on this side!) and off the steps at the end to Queen's Parade Place. Carry on downhill by the road just to the right, keeping left of the trees to the corner of leafy Queen Square. Walk down the west side, cross Chapel Row and carry on ahead along Princes St. At the fork turn left and proceed along gorgeous Beauford Square, passing the ornate northern elevation of the Theatre Royal. Turn right at the next junction, past the refurbished theatre and along Westgate St, turning sharp left (where two roads run parallel) back into the commercial area. After 100m, turn right down Stall St.

Swing left between the columns to the Roman Baths and Grand Pump Room complex, the source of Bath's wealth and fame. Ahead rises the abbey, the last great medieval cathedral built in England. It lay in ruins for 70 years after the Dissolution of the Monasteries and has been much remodelled over the years – the signature flying buttresses did not appear until the 1830s.

Cross the square to the south and head down Church St to Abbey Green, dominated by a magnificent plane tree.

Bear left along North Passage (passing Sally Lunn's bun emporium) to the open square at the end, and then right down the traffic-clogged, ruler-straight Pierrepont St. Aim for the distinctive blue clock of Bath Spa station at its end and go through one of the archways left of the station. Cross the footbridge over the River Avon, turn left by roaring traffic and drop down the path leading to a bridge over the Kennet & Avon Canal. Cross and follow the river upstream (eventually upon a peaceful, dedicated path) to return to the Georgian splendour of Bath and the horseshoe-shaped weir beneath Pulteney Bridge, this striking feature dating from the early 1970s. Take the steps by black railings right of the bridge to return to the street.

Backwater Bath

Distance 6km Time **2 hours**
Terrain **almost everything – city streets,
gravel towpath, woodland path and open
fields** Map **OS Explorer 155** Access **main
line rail and buses from all directions –
Bath is not hard to get to**

**From the narrow boats on the Kennet &
Avon Canal to Bathwick Woods and an
eccentrically marked viewpoint, discover
another side of Bath among its sleepy and
salubrious backwaters.**

Set out from the fountain in the middle
of Laura Place. Walk down Great Pulteney
St, Bath's most elegant boulevard, to its
end by the Museum of Art. Swing left
along Sydney Place, cross the junction
with Bathwick St and branch right along
Beckford Rd. Bend right on the bridge over
the railway tracks and then branch
immediately to the left onto the broad

towpath of the Kennet & Avon Canal. A
delightful 1.25km unwinds in the company
of joggers, dog walkers and the colourful
residents of the moored narrow boats.

At the stone Candy's Bridge spanning the
canal (numbered 184), jump over the stile on
the left; head over the bridge and up the
rising Meadow Lane to its end. Turn right
onto leafy Bathampton Lane, following it
the short way to busy Warminster Rd. Cross
straight over to the hedgerow-lined track
reaching up to the wooded hillside. Pass
through the gate by the waterworks
building and into the woods, taking the
obvious path up the slope.

As the trees thin out and open down
beckons, bear right with the path towards
the radio mast. Pick up the stony track
contouring between Bathwick Wood and
the manicured grounds of Bath Golf Club.
After 500m, passing right of the clubhouse,

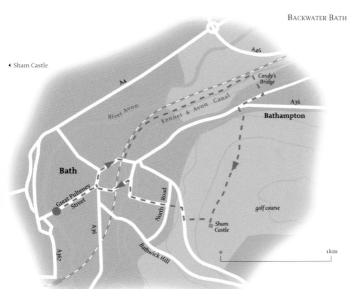

◄ Sham Castle

the remarkable folly of Sham Castle is revealed ahead.

Beside the 'castle', a fine view opens over the city. The eccentric building itself, amounting to little more than screen walls flanking a central arch and turrets, has the air of a stage set. Built in 1762 by Ralph Allen it was never intended to be anything more, its purpose being simply to make the view of the hillside more picturesque when seen from the city streets.

Facing away from the front of the castle, move a little right and turn down the slope on a path at the edge of the woods. Cut across the access road to the golf club and go through the kissing gate opposite. Steeply descend the parcel of National

Trust land to another kissing gate, out onto North Rd, and turn right. After 100m, bear off down the path to the left, at first grassy, then tightly sandwiched between walls, beyond which rise grand Italianate villas. Continue straight over Cleveland Walk and down Sham Castle Lane. Follow this through a narrow section and then bend sharp right to find yourself on a bluff above the canal. Continue along the road to the T-junction at Sydney Rd. Turn left, returning over the canal and the train tracks, and then curve right onto Sydney Place. Cross at the junction with Darlington St, swinging right and then immediately left to return down Great Pulteney St.

Woods and valleys by Castle Combe

Distance 9.5km **Time** 2 hours 45
Terrain woods, pastures, meadows and a
golf course – the full variety of the English
countryside – walking boots are a good
idea **Map** OS Explorer 156
Access Chippenham has the nearest
railway station, with buses (35/35A) from
there to Castle Combe

You have turned the calendar, completed
the jigsaw and watched the period
television drama – Castle Combe is
somehow familiar. Seeing it in the stone
for the first time you have to concede it is
beautiful – harmonious and handsome in
the way only a Cotswold village can be.
The surrounding, deeply folded landscape
– rising here, falling there, hiding secret
paths and opening vistas – is just as
interesting and with none of the
coach party crowds.

Start at the large car park off Dunns Lane,
northeast of the village centre. Head down
the road towards the village. Bear right at
the junction and then right again after 75m
onto School Lane. Follow this past Combe
House and through a grand gateway to its
end, where you turn left into the grounds
of Manor House Golf Club. An obvious
path clings to the fence and then emerges
by a fairway; keep left to pass a green and
dive into foliage. Drop down, curving right
with the wall at the bottom back to the
open playing area. Stick with the path
cutting across the slope beneath the
fairway and down to the roadway. Bear
right, and then left over the bridge,
keeping with the cart track for 100m
to a path leaving by the tee to the
left. Turn off into the woods and
amble along to perhaps the
most elegant kissing

gate you will ever see. Take the path cutting between the converted mill buildings to the left back into the woods (damp and shady even in the height of summer). At the junction with a bridleway, swing left and cross a simple stone clapper bridge. Rise up a trenched, wooded path curving up to the plateau to join a delightful tree-lined lane running to a minor road.

Turn left along the road, sweeping in graceful curves through woodland. Immediately after a junction, branch right onto the path heading south (SP Ford). Emerging out onto a terrace along the rim of a deep, sinuous valley, keep high for around 300m and then rake down to the floor. Cross the stream and maintain your bearing over a meadow and back into trees to reach the head of a stone track, Park Lane. Follow this to the roaring A420 through Ford.

Bear left for only 50m by the traffic, before taking the side road signposted for Castle Combe. Climb this until the woodland falls away to the right and join the footpath contouring the valley side. Hop over a stile to the fenced edge, bear right into woods and descend the sunken lane to the cluster of beautiful houses

tucked into the folds at Long Dean. Bear left at the letterbox and head up the road, its surface soon fading into a rough track. Climbing easily, swing right at the fork to re-enter trees, gaining a terrace carved from the valley side which ducks in and out of copses. Stick with the path – part of the Macmillan Way – to the arched bridge over By Brook and the road just beyond (The Street). Bear right up into the village to the market cross. After a wander, continue up The Street to return to Dunns Lane.

◀ Rustic charm, Castle Combe

Classical Dyrham

Distance 4km (not including any walking within Dyrham Park) **Time** 1 hour 15 **Terrain** largely pasture and grazing land, narrow roadways and cultivated land **Map** OS Explorer 156 **Access** no direct public transport to start

Dyrham Park, a Baroque mansion set in a sleepy bowl north of Bath, is a highlight of the Cotswolds' southern reaches. Most visitors stick to the house and parkland, but that is to overlook an immediate area steeped in ancient history. After exploring the managed parkland, the rougher edges of the surrounding landscape make for a fascinating counterpoint.

It is not necessary to do so to complete the walk outlined here, but making the

most of the National Trust's facilities at Dyrham is highly recommended – free to members, otherwise there is a fee (you can buy tickets to access just the park). The parkland is well worth exploring in its own right – and when open a visit to the house is a must – but it also solves the parking problem, which is otherwise acute. A shuttle bus sometimes runs between the car park and house (useful on the uphill return) and the Trust provides a free leaflet with a couple of nice alternative routes to the driveway down to the front of the house.

The walk begins by the iron gates at the end of the public road just south of Dyrham Park (the house). Walk away from the house, turning right down the wooded

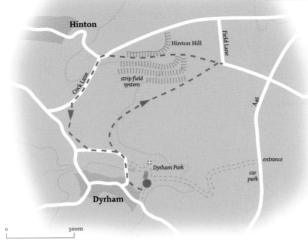

bridleway after 100m. At the end, swing right along the walled Upper Street to pass the impossibly elegant West Front of Dyrham Park, dating from 1692, resplendent beyond immaculate lawns. Follow the road around the bend and then branch off after 75m onto a trenched path (SP Cotswold Way) rising through the wooded verge to open pasture.

Keep right and follow the top edge of this and the subsequent fields. To the left (north) the land initially falls away and then rises up to Hinton Hill, creating the impression of a bowl, the slopes lined by prominent strip lynchets, a prehistoric system of terraces used to improve yields. Entering a usually cultivated fourth field the gradient levels out; after 300m, close to the far end by Field Lane, look for a foot-worn path cutting sharply back to the left

(west). Follow this to the flank of Hinton Hill and continue west along a terrace tucked between hedgerow and the grass rampart of the ancient fort cresting the hill, a fine view opening west over the gently rolling landscape. It is believed that the Battle of Deorham took place here in 577AD, a victory of great strategic importance for the Saxons over the Celts and West Britons.

At the road, bear left and then left again to descend steep Cock Lane (a 'cock' apparently being the extra horse needed to haul carts up the hill). Branch left after 400m onto a path dropping down to level ground and then south across a couple of small pastures to Upper Street. Bear left along the road to retrace the outward route to Dyrham Park, calling in at the handsome St Peter's Church if you wish.

Around Horton Court and Hawkesbury

Distance **8km** Time **2 hours 15**
Terrain **largely peaceful lanes, some stony, some metalled, with a little pasture and woodland; one relatively steep descent**
Map **OS Explorer 167** Access **bus (84, 86) from Bristol and Wotton-under-Edge**

The 'history-o-meter' is sure to twitch and jump on this charming journey along the sleepy lanes straddling the Cotswold Edge, hopping between ancient churches, a famed manor house and a bold monument to military derring-do.

Start out from Hawkesbury Upton Parish Hall. Turn right and follow the High Street west for 125m to the opening just beyond Beaufort House. Turn in and immediately swing right along the track by the field edge, passing some waterworks buildings, to reach Bath Lane – a wide stone track. Bear left to amble south on the level past arable fields. With the edge of the escarpment just off to the west, fine views open ahead and to the right.

Approaching Highfield Lane, branch right, following the inside of the field edge parallel to the road and ignoring any tracks breaking off to the right. By a dilapidated barn, begin to slant down the hillside (guided by Cotswold Way markers), undulating over mounds and into a handsome beech wood. Walk within the top edge of the trees, then descend with the path to an open pasture extending down to the minor road weaving past Horton Court.

Turn right, continuing down into a picture-perfect hamlet brimming with history. Horton Court appears to the right after the first farmhouse, set back down a hedge avenue. In the ownership of the National Trust since the 1940s – but only

knolls, look for a footpath up some steps to the right and then cutting through the fields to lead directly to the side of the yew- and box hedge-decorated churchyard of St Mary the Virgin. For such a small community this is a surprising grand building, hinting at a historical significance now gone. It has a particularly imposing tower, parts of which – as in Horton Court – can be traced back to the 12th century.

Cross the road and head up the lane opposite, rising to skirt the side of Hawkesbury Knoll, then dipping between tightly enclosing hedgerows before climbing once again to a junction with a minor road. Turn uphill and ascend quite sharply towards the Somerset Monument (not initially in view), an Italianate tower built in 1846 to commemorate Lord Somerset, a general at the Battle of Waterloo, which rises elegantly, if a little incongruously, from the Cotswold Edge. To finish, follow the High Street east back into Hawkesbury Upton.

recently, and then quite rarely, opened to the public – the house principally dates from the 16th century, though at its core is a Norman hall. Follow the perimeter wall around, continuing past the slightly elevated St James the Elder, the handsome parish church adjoining the manor house. Set back among the trees behind the church is a fishpond of similarly medieval origin.

Follow the road north (it's generally very quiet and peaceful) for 1.75km, passing Upper Chalkley Farm and then ascending to round the flank of Broad Hill. Approaching Hawkesbury, another hamlet with a prominent church and set beneath wooded

Tyndale's outlook

Distance 9km **Time** 2 hours 45
Terrain lanes, woodland trails and open
escarpment **Map** OS Explorer 167 or 168
Access limited buses (201) from Gloucester
and Thornbury, (311) from Wotton-under-
Edge and Thornbury and (626) from Bristol
and Wotton-under-Edge

**Soaring from the western edge of the
Cotswolds, the Tyndale Monument is a
fine objective for a walk. For a combination
of pastoral beauty, historical interest and
far-reaching views, wind up from tranquil
Waterley Bottom to the escarpment top,
taking in the spurs of Coombe Hill and
Wotton Hill on the way.**

Bisected by the busy B4060, the start
point of North Nibley hardly hints at what
is to come. From the Black Horse Inn, walk
northeast along Barrs Lane. By the speed
limit sign at the village edge fork right (SP
Waterley Bottom), then do the same 500m
on approaching the hamlet of Pitt Court,
remaining on the sleepy road as it sinks
ever deeper into the valley. Drop to the
crossroads in Waterley Bottom, turn right
(SP Wotton-under-Edge) and, beyond the
house, take the path on the left through
the foliage which crowds the bank above
the recessed road. Shadow the road into
fields, keeping to the bottom edge to
emerge at a metal gate back onto the lane.
This leads you uphill before dropping to

pass a large farmhouse. Opposite its straggly
outbuildings, an enclosed footpath leaves
the road to the left. Follow this beneath
powerlines and into Laycombe Wood,
ascending sharply along a trenched path to
an obvious fork. Go left, cross Old London
Road and pick up the path opposite. After
250m go through the kissing gate into
Coombe Hill, a
glorious grassy terrace steeply overlooking
Wotton-under-Edge.

Admiring the ripples of a remarkable
series of strip lynchets, curve around the top
of a rounded spur and the hollow beyond to
a more pronounced promontory with a fine
outlook over the town. Return a short way
to the
right and branch left along a track running
northwest into woods. Keep left at any forks.
Drop over a minor road (Adey's Lane) and
join the path opposite, contouring along the
top of Conygre Wood for 600m to another
distinct fork. Bear right and cross back over
Old London Road to a path cutting left by a
small, disused quarry. Follow the trail a short

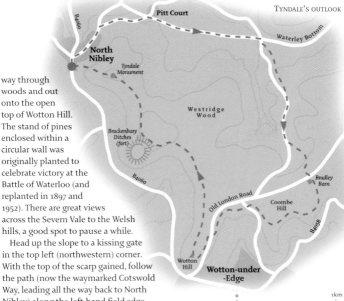

way through woods and out onto the open top of Wotton Hill. The stand of pines enclosed within a circular wall was originally planted to celebrate victory at the Battle of Waterloo (and replanted in 1897 and 1952). There are great views across the Severn Vale to the Welsh hills, a good spot to pause a while.

Head up the slope to a kissing gate in the top left (northwestern) corner. With the top of the scarp gained, follow the path (now the waymarked Cotswold Way, leading all the way back to North Nibley) along the left-hand field edge, then along the inside edge of a wood, before plunging into Westridge Wood proper. At a series of forks go first left, then branch right and left, all the time staying with the Cotswold Way markers. Pass right of Brackenbury Camp, an Iron Age fort, though there is little to see other than the remains of some banks and ditches. Curve right with the path out of the trees and onto the flat, open top of Nibley Knoll and towards the Tyndale Monument. Even from a distance, this first view of the memorial, rising from the windswept escarpment like a Venetian campanile, is unforgettable.

A typical expression of Victorian confidence, the tower was completed in 1866 in memory of William Tyndale, a local scholar. Tyndale was responsible for the first direct translation of the Bible into English and had copies illicitly printed in Antwerp. This was more controversial than it may seem today. Perceived as a troublemaker by the Church authorities, he was burned at the stake in 1536. Those comfortable with claustrophobia-inducing spaces may ascend the steps inside for the remarkable 360-degree view from the top.

Return the short way to North Nibley by a path descending sharply through woodland to a lane out to the B4060.

Uley's hills with history

Distance 8km **Time** 2 hours 30
Terrain a mix of firm, springy upland
grass and potentially muddy lanes
Map OS Explorer 167 or 168 **Access** bus
(21, 35) from Stroud and (35) from Cam
& Dursley Station

**The heights above Uley are steeped in
history, from ancient Uley Bury hill fort to
lonely Downham Hill, once known as
'Smallpox Hill'. Factor in Cam Long Down,
an elegantly tapered ridge, and here is an
upland trio of great character.**

Start by the whitewashed Old Crown Inn
on the B4066 at the eastern end of Uley.
Cross the main road and turn up the
footpath before the grounds of St Giles'
Church. Just past the church itself, branch
right on a path up to a kissing gate at the
base of open pasture. Head directly up the
slope, rising to the edge of trees. Trend left
into the woods and up to a gate. Continue

up and ahead to gain the top of Uley Bury,
keeping right to follow the ramparts to their
northern corner. This prehistoric hill fort,
cut into a promontory of the Cotswold
escarpment, is perhaps the best example of
its type in the area, with evidence of
occupation from 300BC to 100AD. It is
unusually large too, extending to 13 hectares
with ramparts 1.6km long. The wonderful
view over the valley, Downham Hill and the
Severn Vale makes clear the strategic value
the location must once have had.

From the northern corner, drop right on
a track leading back down to the B4066. At
the roadside parking area bear left (west),
joining the Cotswold Way along a trenched
path through woodland. Pass the farm at
Hodgecombe, following the farm lane to a
minor, hedgerow-lined road. Turn right
towards Cam Long Down, which appears as
a squat cone from this angle. At the next
bend, enter the field to the left and ascend

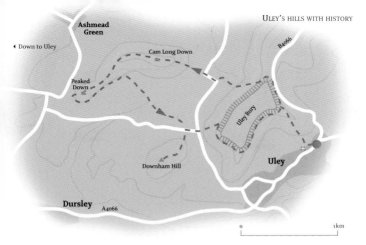

sharply to a line of trees; cut across the contouring path and join a zigzagging trail up to the top.

Follow the apex of the ridge as it narrows and turns to the southwest – the sense of elevation here is out of all keeping with the hill's modest height (220m). Descend off the end into a wooded hollow and up the short way to Peaked Down, a grassy pyramid (decorated with a metal prong) overlooking Cam and Dursley.

Drop steeply west before swinging back to the east above a line of trees skirting the foot of the hill. Cut straight over the Cotswold Way and carry on ahead along a recessed path to a narrow walled bridleway curving around to the southeast. Keep right as this opens out into a track and then, where the track bends right, continue ahead onto another narrow, potentially muddy trail (SP Public Bridleway).

Reaching a road after 500m, veer right and then almost immediately turn left through a metal kissing gate to the permissive path up Downham Hill. This is a straight up and down, primarily along a wide green rake curving up the northeastern edge of the hill to meet an avenue of trees running the length of the top. The hill is open access land with 360-degree views and a colourful history. The hollows at the top are believed to be the remains of an isolation 'hospital' established at the time of the Black Death in the 14th century.

Return to the road and turn right. Continue ahead at the kennels onto a track. Curve to the right and then take the footpath rising to the left, just beyond the driveway to Hydehill. Slant back up to the ramparts of Uley Bury and bear right, making an anti-clockwise round of the impressive fort to return to the eastern corner. Descend to the path through the woods, retracing the route to Uley.

23

Woodchester shadows

Distance 5km Time 1 hour 30
Terrain mainly solid tracks, though some
potentially muddy paths
Map OS Explorer 168 Access Cotswold
Green bus (35) from Stroud to Nympsfield,
600m south of start

**Woodchester Park is at its most haunting
on a crisp winter's day as dusk falls. In the
cold, still air of a tightly enclosed valley,
dark shadows fall in and off the intact but
unfinished shell of this Gothic mansion,
mysteriously abandoned with intricately-
carved fireplaces and doorways hanging in
mid-air and nightmarish gargoyles in
silhouette against the sky – a wonderland
for ghost-hunters.**

The house is owned by the National
Trust and has numerous well-marked
trails. Starting at the information board at
the National Trust car park, 600m north of
Nympsfield and 300m south of the B4066,
take the steps down a tree-fringed bank to a

track. This leads down into the mouth of
the valley, the steep, almost entirely
wooded sides making the already narrow
incision into the escarpment seem
particularly dark and enclosed. Some
plantings date back to the deer park of the
house that preceded the current mansion,
while further east there is a profusion of
dense, post-war conifers. The National
Trust cleared the open pastures to the right
for grazing in the mid-1990s. After 800m, as
the track bends sharply to the left, the
mansion comes into view, a fine example
of the Gothic Revival and apparently
complete. It is only up close that the bizarre
disconnect between the exterior and the
emptiness within becomes apparent.

No one knows why construction came to
a halt. William Leigh purchased the estate in
1845, demolished the existing house and set
to work on a fine building in the then
fashionable style. A perfectionist who
demanded the finest craftsmanship, his

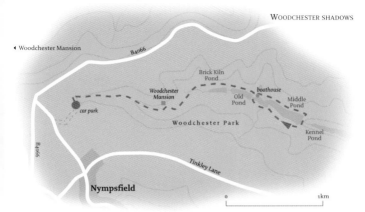

build was the subject of a laborious process, but it is likely that work had already stalled before his death in January 1873. Had the money run out? Did he realise that the dank valley would be detrimental to his poor health? Or something more sinister?

After looking around the exterior (on select days the interior is open), set off to explore the down-at-heel charm of the landscaped park. Follow the carriage drive curving away from the front of the mansion. Keep with the track through parkland for 500m, with a developing sense of seclusion as the trees begin to encroach once again. Pass above the tiny and murky Brick Kiln Pond, the first of five man-made lakes created in the valley bottom in the middle of the 18th century, then by a marker post (with orange arrow) drop down steps to the bank of the next, Old Pond. Go through a black metal gate and wander among the trees to the dam at its eastern end.

Curve slightly up by a stand of tall pines,

then branch right by another orange arrow on an attractive path which passes beneath the tree-lined Honeywell Pond. Middle Pond, the third and largest in the main chain of lakes, is glimpsed between the branches. Continue to the dam at the end of Middle Pond, cross this and take the second gate on the right (not the one for the angling club).

A green track takes you up through open pasture towards tightly packed conifers; by a dip, slant down to a gate in the corner of the field just above the pond. Follow the water's edge (partially along duckboards) to the grassy dam of Old Pond. Cross to the small *Hansel & Gretel*-style boathouse at the other end. Bats roost in the eaves both here and in the mansion, emerging at dusk.

Rejoin the path, following the northern edge of Old Pond to retrace the route back to and beyond the mansion, with – if you have timed your walk for the end of the day – a growing thrill of foreboding as you return through the darkening woods.

The Golden Valley

Distance 9.5km **Time** 3 hours
Terrain woodland paths, open pasture
(possibly cultivated) and former towpath,
with some perilous drops by the locks
Map OS Explorer 168 **Access** bus (54, 54A)
from Stroud and Cirencester

It is said that Queen Victoria bestowed the
name 'The Golden Valley' upon the Frome
Valley near Sapperton. Perhaps she had in
mind the local honey stone buildings, the
setting sun casting a deep, warm light
over the escarpment or the woodland
colours in autumn. Whatever inspired the
name, this quiet valley, largely in the
preserve of the Bathurst Estate with
strong links to the Arts & Crafts
Movement, is a delight to explore.

Go through the five-bar gate by the
telephone box opposite St Kenelm's
Church, Sapperton. Walk initially at the field
edge and then along a fenced path between
brambly fringes and into trees. Beyond a
second gate, wander up the valley along the
length of a long, thin field, continuing
ahead at a junction with a path cutting
down the slope. After a third gate, there's a
first view of Pinbury Park ahead on a spur
overlooking the valley. Here, you curve
right onto a terrace rising above

the steepening slope of a side valley. As it
levels out, slant across the fading slope to
meet a metalled driveway by a pond.

Turn down the driveway, keeping left to
crunch along the gravel path alongside the
topiary and garden wall. Architect and
designer Ernest Gimson, and designers
Ernest and Sidney Barnsley, all influential
members of the Arts and Crafts
Movement, settled here with their families
in 1894 'to live near nature'. They
established a famed furniture workshop in
Sapperton, and extended and renovated
the dilapidated Elizabethan house in tune
with their design principles. Later, in the
1930s, poet laureate John Masefield lived at
Pinbury. You can see why it caught their
imaginations – it is a breathtaking setting.

From the corner of the boundary wall
drop down the good path to the valley
bottom, cross the river and follow the path
to the woods on the far side. Weave up
between the trees and out to the gently
sloping edge of the scarp. Keep to the right
of the field and an immaculately tended
polo ground to reach a short line of trees,
the Gloucester Beeches. From the corner,
bear left (south) and follow the edge
of the fields to a lane end.

Jink left through a double metal

gate and, bearing slightly left (SSE), cut diagonally across the level to a gate back into the woods (aim for just right of a protruding, shrubby knot). Descend to a junction of paths and turn right along an undulating trail through the heart of Dorvel Wood, with scattered stands of dense conifers giving way to more open woodland distinguished by soaring pines. Merging with a second path, veer right and descend on this new line out of the woods and down to Dane Lane. Cross to the footpath opposite and traverse a charming, hummocky pasture to another minor road. Cross this to Siccaridge Wood (a nature reserve), following the gently bobbing path through delightful ancient woodland. Cross a path junction and descend, cutting steeply down to the left at a distinct fork.

Back on the tightly enclosed valley floor, cross the brick Whitehall Bridge and turn left along the largely banked towpath between the crumbling ruins of the Thames & Severn Canal (closed in 1927) and the River Frome. Through the dense foliage, nature is slowly swallowing the vestiges of the lock walls and the silted canal

bed. At the second lock, follow the path over a bridge to the north side, passing three further locks to the roadbridge by the Daneway Inn. Cross this and continue on the path opposite. After 500m, the castellated Daneway Portal, the northern end of the forbidding black Sapperton Canal Tunnel, is reached.

Cross the portal to open country and slant right up the slope back to Sapperton. Reaching road, turn left towards the church and then right on a path past the churchyard to return to the phonebox.

The source of the Thames

Distance 5.5km Time 1 hour 30
Terrain **solid towpath, grazed pastures
and cultivated fields; railway line to cross**
Map OS Explorer 168 Access **Coates is
served from both Stroud and Cirencester
by the 54/54A bus (Cotswold Green)**

**When surveying the mighty, churning
water of the Thames from Tower Bridge, it
might be hard to believe that England's
greatest river starts out unnoticed in the
corner of a quiet field in Gloucestershire.
Water combines with history on this lively
walk by the disused Thames & Severn
Canal, passing the stunning Coates Portal,
to the official source of the Thames.**

Set out from the Village Hall, Coates.
Walk towards the centre of the village,
turning down the footpath to the left
opposite the phonebox by May Tree Close.
Follow the path west through fields, across
a minor road and on to a concrete access
lane. Walk to its end and then branch left

into the field, keeping right of the
farmshed complex. Follow the left-hand
edge through the first field before cutting
slightly to the right through the second
and third fields and dipping down to the
railway line. Exercising extreme caution,
hop over the mainline tracks to the kissing
gate opposite.

Drop through the field to the car park of
the Tunnel House Inn and then turn down
the steps to the towpath of the disused
Thames & Severn Canal and the classical,
colonnaded Coates Portal. A fine example
of Georgian stonework (restored in 1976), it
is certainly the most ornate canal tunnel
entrance in the country and an elegant
counterpoint to the ominous black void at
its heart. The portal marks the southern
end of the Sapperton Canal Tunnel, which
at the time of its opening was the longest
in England. Closed since 1911, there is today
a rather forlorn air to the wooded cutting,
the canal still holding a pool of dark water.

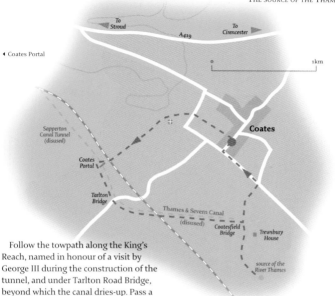

◄ Coates Portal

Follow the towpath along the King's Reach, named in honour of a visit by George III during the construction of the tunnel, and under Tarlton Road Bridge, beyond which the canal dries-up. Pass a lock and the shell of the Coates Roundhouse, one of five lengthman's cottages along the canal. The building once had a bowl-shaped roof (long gone) to collect rainwater. Continue beneath the railway bridge, with the canal bed becoming much more overgrown and frequently disappearing within tangled thickets, to Coatesfield Bridge.

Turn off the towpath to a lane to the right. Follow this to its end and into a pasture. Keeping left, enter a second field to reach (after 150m) the commemorative stone marking the Source of the Thames, tucked in the shade of a stately tree. It is likely that not much (if any) water will be in evidence, but a depression with a small stone circle perhaps marks the likely source of the 'spring'. It is, anyway, the official source, as declared by the Conservators of the River Thames in 1974, and the start/end point of the Thames Path, which snakes its way for 294km to the Thames Barrier at Greenwich. London does indeed feel a long way from here.

Return to Coatesfield Bridge and cross. Rise to a field, keeping with its right-hand edge to a stone stile in the top corner (by a square plantation). Over this, follow the edge of a second field up to Trewsbury Road. Turn left to return to Coates.

29

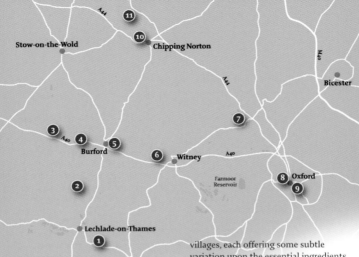

East into Oxfordshire the landscape smooths and flattens, the valleys sitting progressively wider and shallower. With this, the interest drifts from the contours of the land to the way those natural patterns have been deployed and built upon. History rises at every turn – great estates, riverside ruins, artistic boltholes, wartime fortifications – culminating in the outpouring of power and wealth at Blenheim Palace, where Capability Brown re-imagined and re-ordered the natural into a park both breathtaking and bombastic in equal measure.

Two great rivers, the infant Thames and its tributary, the Windrush, weave between arable fields, lazy pastures and scattered woodland, the Windrush Valley presenting a string of uniformly golden villages, each offering some subtle variation upon the essential ingredients of the English village – the village green, church tower, manor house, rough-hewn cottages and public house. The town of Burford is the jewel in this particular crown, the broad avenue of its High Street rising steeply from the medieval humpback bridge spanning the river.

The water leads inevitably to Oxford, where one of the world's great universities goes hand in hand with an astonishing concentration of architectural splendour, relics of past achievement yet alive with youthful potential. If the air here is too refined, seek out the less cerebral pleasures of Chipping Norton, a smart but unpretentious market town, and the prehistoric Rollright Stones, unheralded and almost unnoticed but third only in their significance to Stonehenge and Avebury.

Bliss Mill, Chipping Norton ▸

The East

Kelmscott and the Isis

Distance 7km **Time** 1 hour 45
Terrain riverbanks, village lanes and the
odd cultivated field **Map** OS Explorer 170
Access Lechlade is the nearest bus stop,
served from Swindon to Faringdon
(67, Fridays only), Carterton (64), and
Cirencester (77)

**The Isis is the name for the Thames above
Iffley Lock near Oxford. With its rowing
associations, the name is most commonly
in use around the city itself, but properly
alludes to the river all the way back to its
source. This route follows the riverbank
between two fascinating destinations –
Buscot Lock and William Morris' old home
at Kelmscott Manor.**

Starting from the National Trust car park
in Buscot, walk north along the tree-lined
lane towards the weir. As this enters open
ground, branch right to follow a path

trending east at the edge of cultivated
fields to Buscot Wharf which, strangely, is
not by the water. Pass right of the house
to reach its access lane. Turn right and
walk to its end at a corner of the A417.

Bear sharply left and prepare for a
slightly dull tramp to the river, initially
on a diagonal slant across a pair of fields,
then fenced to the side of a third, before
orientating half-left to cut across a
further pasture to a stone track. Continue
along the track in the same direction to
the grounds of the Anchor Boat Club.
Here stood the fondly remembered
Anchor Inn, accessible only on foot or by
boat – a reflection of the former
importance of the river as a transport
artery. Sadly, it was destroyed by a fire in
1980, which also claimed the lives of the
landlord and his partner, and was never
rebuilt. Follow the path left to the boat-

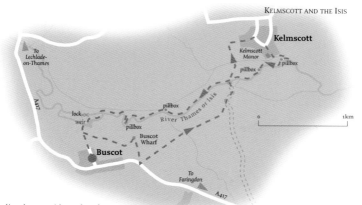

lined waterside and make your way over the river at the elegant Eaton Footbridge.

Jink right and then left, away from the water, heading north through a couple of fields, at the end of the second bearing right down a path tightly enclosed by hedges to the tiny village of Kelmscott. At the road turn right, pass the 17th-century Plough Inn and then fork right after 100m on the lane to Kelmscott Manor. The manor was the country residence of the celebrated writer and designer William Morris from 1871 to his death 25 years. A beautiful building in a fine setting – Morris called it 'a heaven on earth' – its décor is essentially as left by Morris, with furniture, textiles and ceramics of his own design. Owned by the Society of Antiquaries of London, the house is open on selected days in the summer.

Continue along the lane to draw alongside the Thames and then bear right to join the riverside path. There now unfolds a blissfully tranquil 2.5km in the company of sleepy willows and passing motorboats as the river wends its way through the lush Oxfordshire flatlands back to Buscot. Of particular interest, though out of keeping with the riverbank serenity, are the four concrete pillboxes along the way. Built at roughly 600m breaks in 1940, when the fear of Nazi invasion was at its peak, these apparently impregnable bunkers were intended to make the most of the Thames as a natural defensive barrier against enemy forces advancing from the south.

Approaching Buscot, cross the modern bridge over the northern channel of the river and then head up the island to the immaculately-maintained lock. The lock dates from 1790 and is the smallest on the Thames, though it still lets through 55,000 gallons every time it is filled. Cross the lock bridge to another tiny island (with lock-keeper's cottage) and then the bridge over the top of the weir. Follow the path to rejoin the original track, bearing left along this to return to Buscot.

◀ Eaton Footbridge

The Eastleach twins

Distance **7km** Time **2 hours**
Terrain **largely open pasture and
meadow, with a dash of woodland – boots
recommended** Map **OS Explorer OL45**
Access **no direct public transport to start**

The twinned villages of Eastleach Turville
and Eastleach Martin on either side of the
River Leach offer an England of the
imagination – the softly folded landscape,
the sleepy churches and the wisteria-clad
cottages, the shady copses, pea-green
meadows and tail-flicking cattle –
unchanging and timeless.

Set out from the triangular village green,
adjacent to the redundant church of St
Michael & St Martin in Eastleach Martin.
Walk northeast on the minor road

signposted 'Holwell' for 600m to a path
entering the Hatherop Estate via a five-bar
gate. Join a green track curving left along
the foot of the steep valley side, just above
the river. Round a spur, pass through
another gate and follow the edge of woods,
with a line of hawthorns on the other side.
Go left of the wall end and then cross at
the stile 150m on. Continue up the valley
through a couple of open pastures, before
passing left of the majestic lone tree and
down into the woods.

A ribbon of path twists between ivy-
ringed trees to a corner of the wood. Swing
right with the edge and then along an
open channel between wooded banks.
Reaching an obvious 'crossroads', turn left
on a track up the bank and out to the open.

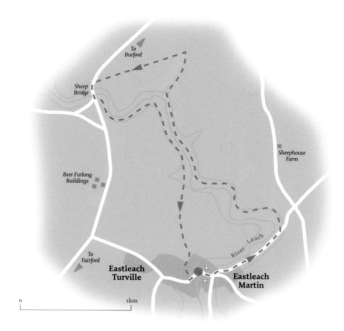

A typically ruler-straight Roman road, Ackeman Street (here just a track), slashes its way across the edge of the scarp and then the short way down to the road, which drops you down to the valley floor with an elegant parkland scene unfolding ahead. Take the second gate to the left, just beyond the river.

A bridleway leads you along the floor of the gracefully curving valley, passing a wooded area before swinging right by an enclosed mound to follow the right-hand field edge. Rising into a second field it leaves the river behind with a view ahead to the villages as you crest the brow.

Keep to the right-hand side into a third field, then slant left to a gate in the far corner. Beyond this, wander down the lane between honey-hued cottages to the road, where you bear left to descend out of Eastleach Turville, across the Leach and back to Eastleach Martin.

◀ Fields above the River Leach

35

A tour of the Sherborne Estate

Distance **5km** Time **1 hour 30**
Terrain **woodland, parkland, estate tracks
and village roads** Map **OS Explorer OL45**
Access **no direct public transport to start**

Nestled in the Windrush Valley just to the
west of Burford, Sherborne is a fine
example of an estate village. While
Sherborne House is in private ownership,
the National Trust has opened up the
surrounding parkland; a tour through the
park and village makes for a fascinating
insight into the make-up of a grand estate.

Start from Ewe Pen Barn, Sherborne
Park (reached 750m from the A40, off the minor
road signposted 'Sherborne and Clapton').
Turn right from the courtyard entrance and
walk east, moving left of the line of trees.

Keeping within the inside edge of the
field, round left down to the corner of the

woods, Ragged Copse. Pick up the trail
weaving between the trees, passing the
carved wooden man and his dog, to a
clearing with another sculpture, a deer
fashioned from old agricultural machinery.
These, and the other sculptures dotted
around the estate, were fashioned with the
help of children from the local primary
school. Continue winding downhill to the
road out to the village.

Bear right along the road. The village is
rather strung out and after the initial run
of workers' cottages there is not much in
the way of development, with a very
pleasant view over to the languid
Sherborne Brook and its neighbouring
meadows. That Sherborne is an estate
village is obvious enough once the
looming stable block (now converted into
homes) appears to the right – there is an

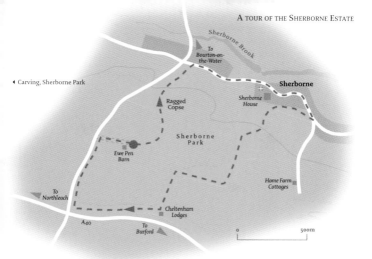

◄ Carving, Sherborne Park

impressively ordered and harmonious air to this, the adjacent lodges, agricultural buildings, imposing perimeter walls and whatever other buildings are dotted around. The epicentre for this, the main house, which has likewise been divided into separate private dwellings, is successfully obscured at this stage by the wall, hedges, trees and other foliage.

Coming to the road junction and war memorial, turn in through the stone gateway in the wall just right of the phonebox. Follow the path through the woods tucked at the foot of rising parkland. Curve upwards, with the main house occasionally peeking into view, staying by a metal fence for as long as possible before re-entering the trees. At a small clearing, an ornate metal seat encircles a yew tree. Continue upwards,

passing just right of the Ice House, before forking left and passing through another metal gate. Weave up through the woods and out to a wide stone track on the level.

Turn right to follow the track, sandwiched between another mighty wall and arable land. Bear left at the junction after 350m to follow the grand Beech Avenue towards the monumental gates – these were once the statement-making start of the principal drive down to the house. Just before the lodges, branch right along a path. Head left towards a bench and back into the canopy of the trees to pick up a sweeping carriage drive running inside the perimeter wall of the estate. It is a delightful way, though until the sharp right bend by the minor road it is in the company of the hum of the A40. Reaching the lodge by the driveway to Ewe Pen Barn, turn right to return to the start.

The timeless Barringtons

Distance **8km** Time **2 hours 30**
Terrain Stony tracks, open pasture and
road; a few ups and downs
Map OS Explorer OL 45 Access no direct
public transport to start

**Honey-hued stone, charming villages
(Windrush, Little Barrington and Great
Barrington), rolling lanes and the patina of
history – it's the Cotswolds in a nutshell.**

Start by the church and village green in
Windrush. Walk east on the road towards
Little Barrington for 100m and then branch
right onto a footpath, continuing in the
same direction across a succession of
pastures. In the fifth field, pass just right of
the knot of trees in the middle before
swinging left down to the road. Bear right
and follow this the short way into Little
Barrington, a particularly attractive village
with a sloping village green bisected by the
road. Turn first left along the no-through

road and then along the path at its end.
Reaching the tip of another lane, bear left
over a footbridge and onto a hedge-lined
path cutting straight up to Barrington Mill.
Go through the yard in front of the building
and up the lane beyond to the public road.

Continue ahead to the west end of the
main drag through Great Barrington,
another sublimely harmonious village.
Cross over, passing the war memorial and
remaining uphill on the road towards Little
Rissington. After 300m, a set of imposing
gates open a view across the deer park of
Barrington Park – a Palladian country
house – to a dome-roofed classical folly.
A further 250m up the road, branch left
along a track cutting across the field (not
the sharper 'no-through road' turn). Lined
by hedges and lush verges, the track now
rolls very enjoyably between arable fields
(the Barrington Park Estate is one of the
largest organic farms in the country),

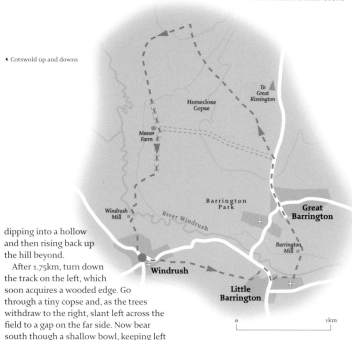

◄ Cotswold up and downs

dipping into a hollow and then rising back up the hill beyond.

After 1.75km, turn down the track on the left, which soon acquires a wooded edge. Go through a tiny copse and, as the trees withdraw to the right, slant left across the field to a gap on the far side. Now bear south though a shallow bowl, keeping left of two copses to meet up with the track rising to Manor Farm, perched on the crest ahead. Skirt left of the farm, with the glorious courtyard to its front seen in retrospect. In an area ripe with fine farmhouses, this is one of the best.

Remain south along the track, following the top edge of the field. Do not go through the gate at the end; instead turn down by the edge to a wooded bank. Through to level pasture, swing left to a five-bar gate, continuing in the same direction through the subsequent field. Pick up the path beyond and curve around to the picturesque Windrush Mill. Just past the mill, turn left in front of a row of cottages to the field at its end. Climb the slope into a second field and look for a walled path to the left. This dips through a wooded glade and passes the edge of another Manor Farm to reach a lane end at the edge of Windrush. Follow this back up to the road, slanting left to return to the village green.

The Windrush Valley

Distance 9km **Time** 2 hours 30
Terrain ups and downs and lots of variety,
from riverside meadows to pastures,
cultivated fields and woodland
Map OS Explorer OL45 **Access** bus (853)
from Oxford and Cheltenham

If the beautiful, evocative name of the
Windrush is something to live up to, the
river and its surrounding valley do not
disappoint. Riverside meadows, historic
pastures and old lanes meet on this
outing from Burford.

Start from Guildenford car park, off
Church Lane in Burford. Cross the bridge
with green railings and swing left on to
Guildenford. At the junction, turn left onto
Witney St; follow the road for 1km, leaving
the town behind (there's either a pavement
or a good verge, except for the final 200m),
to a footpath to the left branching out

across a pasture towards the River
Windrush. The path now traverses a run of
riverside meadows, sometimes brushing
the meandering riverbank, sometimes a
little distant, the way finally constricting
onto a bank running up to a road. Follow
this a short way ahead to the hamlet of
Widford, bearing left along the no-through
road just before the first house (the old
mill). Cross the stone road bridge over the
river and then turn right along the
prominent track 100m on.

This sweeping, tree-dotted field is the
site of the lost village of Widford, believed
wiped out by the Black Death. All that
remains is the 13th century Church of St
Oswald – lonely, simple and rustic.
Continue into a second field and head to a
marker post before turning directly uphill
towards Dean Bottom (avoid cutting the
corner, which only leads to a spring and

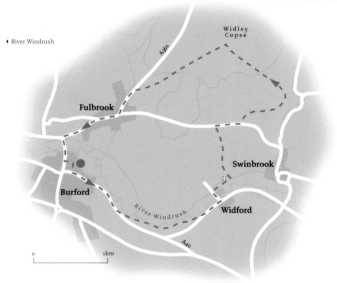

◀ River Windrush

Widley Copse

A361

Fulbrook

Swinbrook

Burford

River Windrush

Widford

A40

0   1km

associated bog). A tiny, narrow valley hemmed in by wooded banks (especially to the coniferous east), Dean Bottom sweeps gently upward in graceful curves – rise within this to its end at a minor road.

Bear right along the road to gain the flat top and then split left along a charming, enclosed lane dipping into a hollow. From its end, a green track slants up the slope ahead to skirt the woods topping Handley Plain (opening a wonderful view), then drops as a stone track to a narrow road. Bear left on the road, climb past Paynes Farm and a final row of houses, beyond which the roadway fractures into a loose track rising (almost imperceptibly) towards a large wood, Widley Copse. At the edge of

the trees, ignore the fork to the right, and continue ahead beneath the dark, overhanging branches.

Emerging into the open within 300m, bear immediately left onto a wide path slashing southwest across a run of three cultivated fields, helped along by a gently falling slope. Reaching the side of the A361 (it is pavement all the way except for the first 100m), turn downhill, through the village of Fulbrook, and on, via the main road, back to Burford. Crossing the medieval stone bridge at the edge of town, linger for a second for a final glimpse of the Windrush, as ahead beckon the pleasures of Burford High Street.

41

The ruins of Minster Lovell

Distance 6km Time **1 hour 30** Terrain some
road walking, but mainly open fields and
pastures Map **OS Explorer 180**
Access **Stagecoach bus (200) from Oxford,
Witney and Carterton to Minster Lovell**

**Ruins make for some of the most
cherished and evocative places in the
English landscape - rich in story and
folklore, they speak of our history and of
the way attitudes towards that has
evolved. Tucked in a romantic spot by the
River Windrush, Minster Lovell Hall, a
15th-century manor house, is perhaps the
most picturesque ruin in the Cotswolds.**

Set out from Wash Meadow Recreation
Ground car park in Minster Lovell. Walk
north into the village, turning right along
the sleepy High Street – which, in the
typical Cotswolds way, is harmony itself
with a number of fine thatched cottages
and immaculately tended gardens. At the
top of the street keep left (ignoring the
branch right to the church) and follow
Crawley Dry Lane out of the village.
Beyond the last house, Manor Farm, bear
off on a footpath into the field to the
right. Slice diagonally across this and
follow the northern edge of a second
field, with the chimney of Crawley Mill
visible ahead. After cresting a low brow,
take the obvious track (Wood Lane) ahead,
rising to a line of cottages etched into the
hillside at the edge of Crawley.

Wander down Farm Lane to the small
village green by the Lamb Inn and turn
right to head south on Dry Lane. Cross the
roadbridge and then look for a footpath
to the left, across from the small business
units at Crawley Mill. Weave along the
valley bottom, sandwiched between
hedgerow 'walls' and, in summer,

◄ St Kenelm's and the ruins of Minster Lovell

towering grasses and cow parsley. After 600m, by a pair of gates, turn right onto a bridleway rising back to the road; cross to a path opposite reaching into trees. Descend a steep, wooded bank back into the valley and traverse a run of pastures.

Enter woods by a disused, brick pumphouse and then keep right at a fork to come to the side of the Windrush. Cross the bridge over the weir back into open pasture with the picturesque ruins in sight ahead – this is much the best line of approach. Explore the impossibly romantic riverside ruins, which are managed by English Heritage. The hall was built in the 1430s by William, Baron Lovell, on the site of an earlier manor house; having fallen out of the possession of the family, the house was abandoned in the 1740s, with the east and west ranges demolished for building stone (though

the footprint of both is still obvious enough). Note the corner staircase cut off in mid-air, and have a competition to find the earliest set of initials carved into the stone – 18th century, if you are doing well. The isolated southwest tower close to the river is a particularly striking survival. English Heritage provides a number of information boards illuminating the story of the hall at greater length. Take the time to also explore the adjacent St Kenelm's, a picture perfect country church, which dates from the building of the hall.

Take the path above the fish ponds (which would have supplied the hall) out of the grounds and alongside a fence into the village, finally crossing back over the recreation ground to return to the car park.

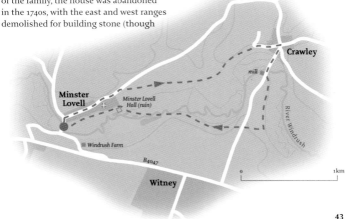

Blenheim unsurpassed

Distance 7.5km **Time** 1 hour 45
Terrain parkland, metalled drives and
solid paths **Map** OS Explorer 180
Access Stagecoach bus (S3) from Oxford
and (242) from Witney to Woodstock;
long-stay car park on Hensington Road

Blenheim Palace needs little introduction.
Seat of the Dukes of Marlborough,
designed by Sir John Vanbrugh and
birthplace of Sir Winston Churchill, it is
Britain's grandest and most flamboyant
country house. If the palace and its
immediate vicinity can become choked
with visitors in summer, the magnificent
park is almost never over-burdened and,
by following the public rights of way, is
free to visit.

Start on the High St in Woodstock,
outside famed hotel, The Bear. Cross the
road and walk along Brown's Lane
(adjacent to The Star Inn) to its end; drop
down steps to the A44 and turn left. Pass

a row of cottages and then go through the
large green-painted gate (No 95) 50m on.
Though it looks like someone's driveway,
do not be deterred; it is a public right of
way. Continue ahead and pass through
the entrance in the wall to the left into
Blenheim Park. Turn right along the
carriage drive; within 100m there is a view
across Queen Pool to the palace. The
Manor of Woodstock was granted to John
Churchill, 1st Duke of Marlborough, by
Queen Anne for his part in the defeat of
the French at the Battle of Blenheim in
Bavaria in 1704, with the promise that the
grateful nation would also provide the
funds to build a grand residence – though
these were exhausted long before the
palace was completed.

Follow the level drive past a cottage and
then up through a narrow, wood-fringed
valley, finally curving up to the plateau.
Here the long avenue of limes opens, a
ruler-straight double-planting perfectly

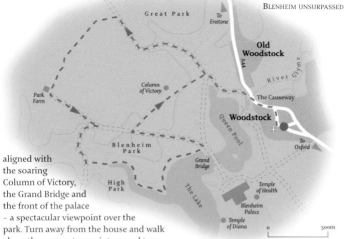

aligned with the soaring Column of Victory, the Grand Bridge and the front of the palace – a spectacular viewpoint over the park. Turn away from the house and walk along the avenue to a point around two-thirds of the way to where a fence cuts across. Branch left at 45 degrees through the trees to a side fence and follow this to a stile. Now head southwest for the length of a long, thin field, keeping right of the copse midway along and then left of the circular knot of trees a further 200m on (ignore the kissing gate to the right).

Picking up a metalled lane, pass left of Park Farm and then bend sharply left along a shaded avenue. After 400m turn right at a road junction and descend between trees into a tiny, hidden valley, dotted with specimen plantings. Beyond a cattle grid turn left onto a path cutting down the valley to a gate. Pass through this and swing right to follow the path by the lakeside, with scenes of studied pastoral elegance unfolding in the company of gliding swans. As the path curves up and away from the water's edge, a wonderful

view is revealed to the full face of Vanbrugh's magnificent Grand Bridge, intended to be the finest in Europe. Upon reaching the drive, turn down for a closer look at the bridge and for a clearer view to the Great Court (note that the public right of way ends just before the bridge).

Turn back up the roadway to the left and look for a stile to the right after around 600m. Following the line of a fence, walk back over grass to the Lime Avenue, which swells to a ring around the Column of Victory, a 40m-high fluted Doric column commemorating the 1st Duke's military victories, among other family achievements. Continue in the same direction and down to a drive fringing the Queen Pool. Turn left to a junction beyond a cottage. Now turn right and retrace the outward route back into the heart of Woodstock.

◀ The Grand Bridge and Blenheim Palace

On the case with Morse

Distance 2.5km Time 1 hour
Terrain city streets and solid gravel paths
Access start point is 750m east of the railway station and 150m northeast of the Gloucester Green bus station; parking in Oxford is difficult and very costly – try the park & ride

Oxford may be home to one of the world's finest universities, but for years it was a city best known as a hotbed of vengeful academics, spurned wives, and greedy con-artists. Chief Inspector Morse took the ensuing murder rate in his stride – now follow his example.

Begin your investigations at the end of Beaumont St, by the junction with St Giles'. To one side is the Randolph Hotel, to the other the imposing neoclassical front of the Ashmolean, the university museum of art and archaeology. Both feature in 'The Wolvercote Tongue', which weaves together a suspicious death in the hotel with the donation of an artefact to the museum. (Drawn from the novels of Colin Dexter, the *Inspector Morse* television dramas were broadcast between 1987-2000.)

Walk south on Magdalen St, continuing over the junction onto Cornmarket St. To the left, by the Church of St Michael at the North Gate, the murderous don at the end of 'The Last Enemy' meets his doom.

Take the second road to the left, Market Street, and make your way into the covered market, a venerable Oxford institution. The building opened in the 1770s and has a

QVOD FELICITER VORTAT
ACADEMICI OXONIENS
BIBLIOTHECAM HANC
VOBIS REIPVBLICAEQVE
LITERATORVM
T. B. P.

wonderfully old-fashioned feel. In 'Greeks Bearing Gifts' Morse undertakes a surprisingly energetic chase through here. Continue along Market Street and turn right onto The Turl (in the other direction is Exeter College, whose Front Quad is the setting for Morse's final moments), one of Oxford's most atmospheric streets with the Lincoln College library – a converted Romanesque church – dominating.

Cross the High St (Morse drove along here dozens of times, Wagner rising at full blast from the windows of his old crimson Jaguar) and walk down Alfred Street to The Bear pub. Morse drinks and ruminates here in 'Death is now my Neighbour'. The tiny pub is notable for a remarkable collection of almost 5000 neckties (mostly club, school and regimental). Turn right and follow peaceful Blue Boar Street to the hubbub of St Aldate's, turning left. Pass the entrance to Christ Church, perhaps the grandest college of all, and then turn left through the gates to the lavender-edged path through the college War Memorial Gardens. Continue ahead onto Broad Walk, a gravel drive between the south front of the college and the edge of the pastoral Christ Church Meadow.

Bear left on a path by the railings around Merton sports field and walk up to the old city wall, passing through a turnstile to a shaded path (Grove Passage) at the side of Corpus Christi College. Cross Merton St and head up the narrowing Magpie Lane opposite; cross back over the High Street and curve left of the University Church of St Mary the Virgin ahead to reach Radcliffe Square. Here, the university's great architectural set piece unfolds. How many times did Morse and Lewis stroll (and drive!) this way, pondering leads and suspects with the Radcliffe Camera, the circular domed building in the centre of the

◀ 3rd Earl of Pembroke, Bodleian Library

The Cherwell by Christ Church Meadow ▶

square, as their backdrop? Built in the 1740s in the Palladian style, this remarkable building is today a reading room of the Bodleian Library.

To the left is Brasenose College, which posed as the fictional Lonsdale College on numerous occasions. Move clockwise around the rotunda to Catte St. Swing left and then turn left through the Great Gate into the Bodleian's Old School Quadrangle for a close-up slice of the splendour and history of the university. Morse walks through here in 'The Setting of the Sun', pausing to look up at the statue of university benefactor, the 3rd Earl of Pembroke. Pass through the archway to the north to the courtyard facing the exquisite Clarendon building ahead and with the dome-topped Sheldonian Theatre to the left. Here, in 'Twilight of the Gods',

opera diva (and Morse favourite) Gladys Probert is shot by a sniper.

Leave through the gates to the east and continue ahead to pass beneath Hertford Bridge, aka the Bridge of Sighs, over New College Lane, before turning left down the twisty St Helen's Passage to discover the Turf Tavern, one of the Inspector's favourite destinations for a cheeky pint.

Bear left in front of the pub around to Bath Place and up to Holywell St. Turn left and continue over the junction to Broad St, calling in at Blackwell's, the city's largest and oldest bookshop, where Morse conducts an interview in 'Who Killed Harry Field?'. Continue along Broad St, familiar from dozens of scene-setting tracking shots, back to the corner of Cornmarket and Magdalen Streets, turning right to return to the Ashmolean. Case closed!

The parks of Oxford

Distance **7.5km** Time **2 hours**
Terrain **city streets and solid gravel paths**
Map **OS Explorer 180** Access **start point is 750m east of the railway station and 150m northeast of the Gloucester Green bus station**

From students pretending to study to single-minded joggers and punting tourists, all shades of Oxford life gather within its greenery. This walk links the University Parks and Christ Church Meadow – all by way of Mesopotamia!
(Note: the gates to the University Parks, Headington Hill Park and Christ Church Meadow are locked at sunset – try not to be caught out.)

Set out from the corner of Broad St and Cornmarket St. Walk east along Broad St, one of the most imposing in the city, past the gates of Balliol College on the left and the Sheldonian Theatre on the right. Beyond Blackwell's Bookshop turn left onto Parks Rd. Peek through the elegant gates revealing the lawns of Trinity College and then look to cross the road, continuing over the junction with South Parks Rd to see two of the country's finest examples of High Victorian Gothic architecture – to the right the University Museum of Natural History and to the left Keble College, with its distinctive patterned brickwork.

At the bend, bear right through Keble Gate into the University Parks. Swing left along the gravel path and walk clockwise around the perimeter of the park. There are many fine specimen trees to be found here, including a Giant sequoia on the

49

corner as the West Walk curves gently round to the North Walk. Many of the finest players to grace the game of cricket have played upon the university's pitch in the centre of the park. In the northeast corner, as the way forks in a wooded dell, branch left and make a round of the tranquil lily pond, in the process coming alongside the River Cherwell.

Walk downstream with the river, keeping left to Cox's Corner and a kissing gate out onto a cycle lane (watch out – it is a racetrack). Head left and then turn off to the right just before the bridge by the weir. Walk a short way downstream and then cross a wooden-framed bridge onto a sliver of land splitting the Cherwell. Extending for 800m, this is known locally as Mesopotamia, the name derived from the Greek for 'between the rivers'. Follow the

obvious concrete path as it runs the length of the island – astonishingly peaceful and rural for somewhere so close to the city centre – to the old mill at its end.

Wander up King's Mill Lane to busy Marston Rd. Cross and pick up a path just to the right, signed 'Cuckoo Lane'. Turn up and then immediately bear right into Headington Hill Park. Follow a gravel path uphill to a metalled drive, then turn right and drift along the level towards an ornate pair of blue gates. Though relatively small, this is a beautiful park: shaded, rolling and spacious. Approaching the gates turn down on a path to the bottom corner. Exit and turn right, cross straight over the hectic junction at London Place and follow St Clement's St, a busy and, within the context of Oxford, slightly humdrum street.

Coming to the roundabout at The Plain

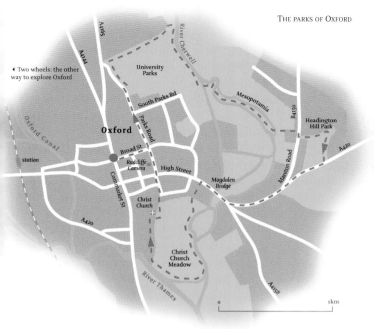

‹ Two wheels: the other way to explore Oxford

keep right and pass alongside the stone balusters of Magdalen Bridge over the Cherwell (it used to be a post-exam tradition for students to jump from here into the water, but it is now discouraged).

Cross the High Street near the Botanic Gardens and turn down the next side road, Rose Lane. Pass through the gates at the end and follow the path ahead to return to the Cherwell. Stay by the water on a glorious winding tour at the edge of Christ Church Meadow – cattle often graze the meadow itself. Reaching the confluence with the Thames (motor boats galore), ignore the bridge and continue alongside

railings to the head of grand poplar-lined New Walk, reaching up to Christ Church.

By the college buildings, turn right on Broad Walk and then left on a path before the railings of Merton sports field. In the corner, go through the turnstile in the old city wall and along the shaded Grove Passage past Corpus Christi College to Merton St. Walk up the narrowing Magpie Lane opposite, cross the High Street and skirt right of the church ahead on to Catte St. Complete the walk by passing Oxford's most famous buildings – the Radcliffe Camera and Bodleian Library – to return to Broad Street.

In and out of Chippy

Distance 4km **Time** 1 hour 15
Terrain largely stone tracks, but some
roadway and pasture **Map** OS Explorer 191
Access bus (S3) from Oxford and (50) from
Stratford-upon-Avon to Chipping Norton

Chipping Norton may have acquired
notoriety for its 'set', but at heart it is a
busy, relatively unpretentious market
town (known locally as 'Chippy').
Combine the town and the low ridge
overlooking it on this short walk, enjoying
a distant view to Bliss Mill – a local
landmark and remnant of past industry.

Set out from the western side (the lower
half) of the market square in the centre of
Chipping Norton and walk north along
Market Street. Turn left onto Church St and
head to its end at the handsome Church of
St Mary the Virgin. Turn right along a path

just before the church, pass through a cycle
barrier and continue ahead along a stone
track curving down to the left. Go through
a kissing gate just to the right of the gate
to 'Spring Hill', and pick up a path winding
through a tiny wooded valley. After
passing under a bridge, the path eventually
rises up to the side of the B4026. Turn
uphill along the shaded verge for the short
climb to the edge of Over Norton.

Coming to the sharp Cleeve's Corner, take
the lane branching left away from the village
(SP Restricted Byway – Salford). The track
contours west across the hillside with a
broad view opening over the town. After
500m, keep left at the fork and begin a very
gentle, rolling descent along a track splitting
cultivated fields, accompanied by a line of
hedgerow to the right. Where the track
bends sharply left towards Elmsfield Farm,

◀ New Street, Chipping Norton

continue ahead to a pair of gates. Facing these, swing left to follow the wooded field edge. Crest the brow and descend through a kissing gate to an access road.

Cross straight over to a thin path and continue down, skirting the residential edge of the town. Hop over a second roadway and descend to the bottom of the valley. Cross a tree-fringed stream and rise directly to the A44 by a playground. For a good view of Bliss Mill cross to the metal kissing gate opposite and walk down the field. The high chimney rises imperiously from a cupola, the elegant, rather ornate totality appearing less like a working

industrial building than an amalgam of a mansion and a folly. Wool and tweed production was its business until it closed in 1980. It is now split into private apartments.

Retrace you steps back to the A44 and turn uphill along the leafy pavement to return to the centre of 'Chippy'.

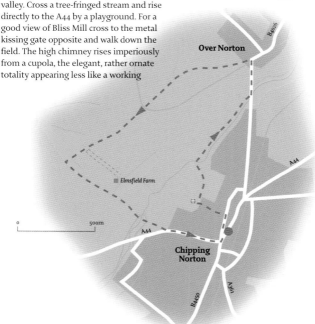

The Rollright Mysteries

Distance 4.5km **Time** 1 hour 15
Terrain a mixture of pasture and
cultivated fields, with some road walking
Maps OS Explorers 191 and OL45
Access infrequent bus services from
Shipston-on-Stour and Chipping Norton
to Long Compton

One of the secrets of the Cotswolds, tucked
away on the Oxfordshire-Warwickshire
border, is a complex of megalithic
monuments, including an ancient stone
circle. Relatively unknown, and modest in
scale, the mystery of the Rollright Stones'
ancient purpose remains unsolved.

It is not an especially promising start: a
lay-by to the side of a minor road, off the
A3400, 1.5km south of Long Compton, in
the middle of largely anonymous arable
fields along the low ridge between the
Stour and Swere Valleys. The first clue is
the green sign at the western end, headed
'The Rollright Stones'. Go through the
adjacent metal kissing gate. Tucked
around to the right, just beyond the stand
of trees, is the King's Men, an early Bronze
Age stone circle. If the 77 irregular
limestone stones appear somewhat
weather-beaten and diminished,
remember the circle dates from 2500-
2000BC. Though hardly spectacular in the
Stonehenge way, there is a vaguely eerie
feeling to the site.

Follow the wide permissive path east
around the edge of the field to the
secluded Whispering Knights, a group of

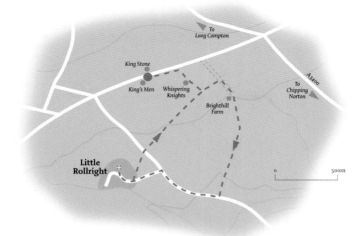

tall stones leaning in conspiratorially and believed to mark a burial chamber.

Continue downhill for another 100m and then bear left to cross a pair of stiles either side of a private track. Follow an avenue through a youthful plantation and turn down the lane at the end. Slip left of Brighthill Farm to a stile out to open pasture. With the low, wide valley reclining and stretching out ahead, bear diagonally right and descend to the bottom corner of the field. Stick to a line clinging to the right-hand side of a pair of fields, and then slant marginally left in a third to reach a gate out to a narrow road.

Turn right and follow the road on a gentle, upward sweep guarded by lines of regimented young trees. After 800m, branch left along the rough, open lane to the tiny hamlet of Little Rollright. Follow this to the simple square-towered 13th-century church of St Philip. Return 150m along the lane and turn up a path rising between lines of immature hedgerow.

Back at the road, cross to the metal five-bar gate opposite and pick up a path slicing northeast across a pair of cultivated fields. Inside the far edge of the second, swing left to return to the Whispering Knights, following the permissive path back to the lay-by. One last detour is to cross the road (which marks the county boundary) to view the final element of the Rollright mysteries, the King Stone, a lone monolith of unknown purpose. It is said that in the 19th century, drovers chipped small bits off the stone to act as lucky charms and to keep the Devil at bay!

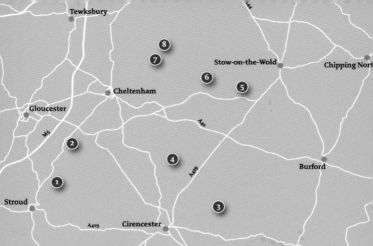

Carved a little more emphatically from the surrounding escarpment, the valleys of the western and central Cotswolds have nurtured their own, sometimes eccentric worlds. Look out for England's cheese-rolling epicentre of Cooper's Hill, the lonely Slad Valley, described with such vim by Laurie Lee, and two of the nicest places imaginable, called 'Slaughter'.

Tucked away between Gloucester and Stroud, but quite separate from either, the compact valleys around Slad and Cranham feel more secluded than they are, due in part to the steep valley sides that enclose them and in part to the woodland that reaches around almost every corner. From soaring beeches to managed coppice, the arboreal delights take many forms; a rewarding dawdle among the trees is never far away.

Arcing northeast there is a more open character to the landscape, reflected in billowing, rounded hills ('wold', after all, is loosely a 'high open land') covered by a dizzying thicket of paths and lanes. These are best experienced on the tops rising around Guiting Power and Winchcombe, where the Neolithic burial chamber at Belas Knap lies hidden. The ancient endures elsewhere within easy reach, at the ruins of Hailes Abbey, dissolved by Henry VIII, and at Sudeley Castle, the resting place of his last wife, Katherine Parr.

To the south, the languid River Coln flows southeast through a shallow valley, past Bibury, considered by William Morris to be 'the most beautiful village in England' and more recently rated (by the American Fox News) as one of 'The World's 16 Most Picturesque Villages'. Further downstream and less well-known, in the charming rolling landscape around Chedworth, are the most complete remains of a Roman Villa in Britain.

Cottages, Bibury ▶

The West

A Slad Valley circular

Distance 7.5km **Time** 2 hours 15
Terrain woodland paths, open down and
roadside – steep and rough in places
Map OS Explorer 179 **Access** very limited
Cotswold Green buses (23, 63) from Stroud
to Slad

The steep, richly textured landscape
around Slad is synonymous with *Cider
with Rosie*, Laurie Lee's enchanting
memoir of growing up in the inter-war
years. Evoking the rustic simplicity and
gentle freedoms of the time, Lee
composes an extended love letter to this
isolated and romantic valley, a delight to
discover then and now.

Start out from the roadside parking area
at Bull's Cross, 1km north of Slad off the
B4070. Head along the road towards Slad,
pass the two adjacent road turnings and
then immediately split right along the
broad path towards Frith Wood Nature

Reserve. A good path leads between the
trees and then emerges into the open,
continuing in the same direction beside a
line of hedgerow. Cross a track and head
down a stony lane, bypassing the eclectic
range of buildings at Worgan's Farm. Just
beyond the main farmhouse, bear left onto
a path meandering down the hillside
alongside a crumbling, overgrown wall at
the edge of woods. Cross the field below
and continue straight down (ignore the
track to the left) to the road.

Turn left and follow the pavement – at
the edge of a twisting terrace hewn from
the hillside, with a fine view over the valley
– north into Slad. Pass the Woolpack Inn (a
Lee favourite) and then branch right after a
further 250m onto Steanbridge Lane. Just
before the turning, look out for the T-
shaped house nestled below the road –
this is Rosebank, the house in which Lee
grew up. Follow the narrow road out of the

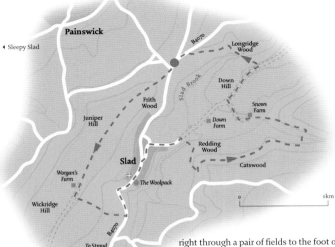

◄ Sleepy Slad

Painswick

B4070

Longridge Wood

Slad Brook

Down Hill

Frith Wood

Snows Farm

Juniper Hill

Down Farm

Redding Wood

Slad

Catswood

Worgan's Farm

The Woolpack

Wickridge Hill

B4070

0   1km

To Stroud

village and down into the bottom of the valley. Immediately beyond a long, low building, turn off to the right (SP Restricted Byway), past a pond and into a field. Ascend to a stile into trees, continuing up to the top edge of the wood before bearing left (don't cross the next stile) along a bobbing path. Meeting a trenched bridleway, turn up and then cut back to the left on a path after 200m. A wonderful terrace now stretches out within the top of Redding Wood, contouring between ivy-wrapped trees (ignore the track forking right). With the view opening across the valley remain on the level along the bottom edge of Catswood. Where a path splits right, locate a stile to the left and descend diagonally

right through a pair of fields to the foot of the 'deep-ditched valley', as Lee puts it. Cross a plank over a stream, a stile and a tiny stone bridge over Dillay Brook and then rise through pasture to pass left of Snows Farm, a nature reserve.

Wander up the surfaced access lane, passing a row of tiny cottages, to a sharp left bend. Branch right, along the track climbing directly up Down Hill. Follow the track along the top of the ridge – with gallops, rings and other horse training facilities to either side – and into Longridge Wood. Reaching a semi-clearing after 150m, bear off to the left on a path weaving sharply down between the trees to a pond. Rise a short way up the far slope and then swing left along a forestry track, which meanders in graceful curves back to the B4070, emerging just a few metres east of Bull's Cross.

59

Cranham and Cooper's Hill

Distance 6.5km **Time 2 hours**
**Terrain woodland paths; steep in places –
boots recommended** Map **OS Explorer 179**
**Access very limited bus service (23) from
Cheltenham or Stroud and (256) from
Gloucester to Cranham; hourly bus (46) to
Cranham Corner on the A46, just over 1km
from the start**

The village of Cranham has a place in the
popular consciousness for two entirely
unconnected reasons. Firstly, in 1904,
Gustav Holst composed a tune while
staying in the village and named it
'Cranham' in honour. Setting a poem by
Christina Rossetti to this, 'In the Bleak
Midwinter' was born and Christmas was
never quite the same again. Meanwhile, at
the far end of the woods to the north of
the village, you find Cooper's Hill, famed
for its hair-raising 'cheese-rolling' race
each spring. Whether midwinter, spring,
summer or autumn, a wonderful, woodsy
adventure awaits.

Set out from the parking area at the foot
of Buckholt Wood, just west of Cranham
off the minor road to the A46. From the
access sign, head up the broad path into
the stately beech wood, following a gently
upward and more or less straight
trajectory. Cross Buckholt Road
(sometimes referred to as Sanatorium
Road) and continue up the path opposite
to a junction of paths at the brow; bear
right (away from the steep slope) and
descend gently to a fork, turning down
sharply alongside a wall.

Levelling out, choose the middle of the
three paths (SP Cotswold Way) – with a
soundtrack rising from the A46 below –
and undulate around a limestone-flecked
crest and on to the coppice beyond. Cut
right at a track, following it between
pastures and through a kissing gate. Swing
left through Brockworth Wood along a
spacious avenue. Jink right over a vehicle
track (following two Cotswold Way signs)
and, 100m on, leave the woods to open

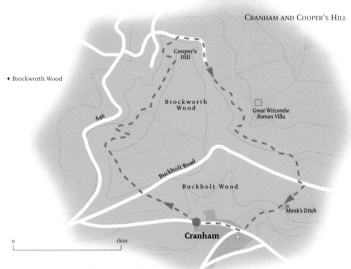

◀ Brockworth Wood

Cooper's
Hill

Brockworth
Wood

A46

Great Witcombe
Roman Villa

Buckholt Road

Buckholt Wood

Monk's Ditch

Cranham

0   1km

ground and the top of the spectacularly steep Cooper's Hill, the UK's cheese-rolling centre. Traditionally contested by the residents of nearby Brockworth, but today drawing interest from around the world, the competitors race headlong down the hill in pursuit of a 4kg Double Gloucester – reckless glory, or gloriously reckless? Go left from the top of the hill back into the words to descend a steepening path; at the rake bear right to the foot of the slope.

Head down to the no-through road and turn right. From the road end, continue ahead on a track into the woods. Tucked just inside the edge of Cooper's Hill Wood stride along the level terrace, with Witcombe Reservoirs peeping in and out of view to the left, passing a final cottage. After a further 600m, at the junction with the path rising directly from the reservoirs

and the Roman Villa, branch right, contouring around a wooded amphitheatre. Continue – soon back by the edge of the trees – for 500m, and then split off to the right along a path rising into the body of Buckholt Wood.

Pass a large house by way of a gravel path and then cross back over Buckholt Road. Drift left through a parking area and descend by the track straight down the slope (not the one bending left) to pass a detached villa, Monks Ditch. The track gives way to a path dipping into a hollow and then rising over a shoulder to the common at the edge of Cranham. Follow the lane to the road and turn downhill, wandering through the village to the valley bottom and then up the short way back to the start point.

Between Bibury and Coln St Aldwyns

Distance 10km **Time** 2 hours 30
Terrain tracks, open pastures and riverside
meadows **Map** OS Explorer OL45
Access bus (855) from Cirencester and
Moreton-in-Marsh to Bibury

**The soft folds, open downs and riverside
pastures of the Coln Valley are the very
essence of the Central Cotswolds
landscape. So, leave the milling summer
crowds behind in Bibury for a couple of
hours of gently undulating exploration.**

Start in the centre of Bibury by the Swan
Hotel. Walk across the stone roadbridge
and walk up the hill towards Arlington.

Take the first turning on the left (Hawkers
Hill), head to the tiny green and bear right
along the unmade lane (SP Ready Token).
Follow the lane to its end, go through the
gate and follow the right-hand edge of
consecutive fields. At the end of the second
swing left onto a lovely old lane,
sandwiched between cultivated fields. The
way leads along the top of the broad ridge
and then drops, enclosed, into a narrow
tributary valley. Rise up the far side to a
five-bar gate on the skyline; head through
this and along the track to the road.

Bear left along the road. Pass the cluster
of cottages and then turn into the field to
the left, picking up a bridleway slanting
right. Pass between the farm buildings
outlying Coneygar Farm, cross the drive
and then cut straight across a pair of
cultivated fields. Hug the top of the next –
which has a distinct, parkland feel – and

descend past an elegant copse towards the stone bridge over the river at the edge of Coln St Aldwyns.

Join the path by the river and head upstream, back towards Bibury. The path soon drifts away from the water, into woods at the edge of the Williamstrip Estate and then along the northern edge of the trees, before returning to the banks of the Coln. Follow the way through a pair of languid pastures and the foot of Ash Copse. At the end of the next field look for a tiny footbridge over the bed of an almost always dried-up stream; cross this and climb the steep, wooded bank beyond to gain a track running along the outer edge of Oxhill Wood. Curve down with the track through a five-bar gate and into open country, with Bibury handsomely displayed ahead. After 250m, cut up on the track to the left and rise to a gate. Skirt right of the idyllically situated cricket pitch and then branch down to the right on a path through woods. Descend to pass the back gardens of Arlington Row, a string of weavers' cottages which represent the much-photographed apotheosis of rustic Cotswold architecture. Cross the footbridge and bear left along the pavement to return to The Swan.

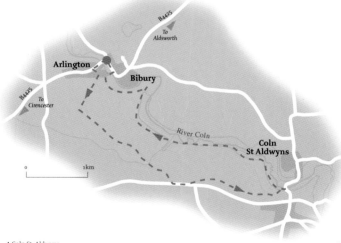

Chedworth foundations

Distance 11km **Time** 3 hours
Terrain tracks, pastures and woodland,
some ups and downs – boots
recommended **Map** OS Explorer OL45
Access limited bus service (854/855) from
Cirencester to the Roman Villa

When, in 1864, a local gamekeeper
stumbled upon fragments of paving in
Chedworth Woods, he couldn't have been
expected to know he had discovered the
remains of what would once have been
one of the largest country houses in
Britain, a Roman mansion with 50 rooms.
Many years of painstaking archaeology
later, the villa is famed for its mosaic
floors and artefacts, bathhouses and 2km
of Roman walls. At the far end of the walk
are foundations of more recent historical
significance, with the strung-out village
of Chedworth and the parkland of the
Stowell Estate along the way.

Set out from the National Trust visitor
centre at the Roman Villa. Take the path up
into the woods, pass beneath a disused
railway line and, 100m on, bear left by a
Macmillan Way marker post. Follow
the path through a hollow and out to the
edge of the trees. A distinct trail now leads
across cultivated fields (ignore any gates)
to a short line of trees and a stepped
descent to a pasture. Drop down and
continue in the same direction, curving
right (just past the encroaching trees) to
a five-bar gate at the edge of Chedworth.

Walk down the lane past St Andrew's
Church to the junction at its end and turn
down to the left. Just before the Seven
Tuns Inn leave right along the public
footpath, looking for a stile to the left into
trees. Hop over this and the line of the old
railway and descend to the stream.
Without crossing, follow it downstream to
a minor road. Turn right and then left
beyond the house onto a path arcing
gracefully around a bend of the valley
before drifting up to the road.

Turn left along the road, taking the fork
left towards Stowell to return to the foot of
the valley. At the sharp left bend after
400m branch right along a footpath
snaking through Hedgley Bottom, a

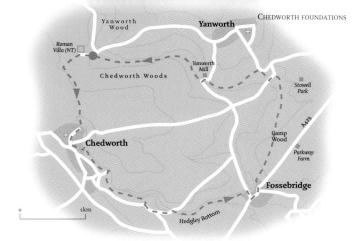

shallow cleft. Emerging at a pasture continue ahead towards houses, swinging right at the field end to reach the roaring A429. Turn downhill, cross Fosse Bridge and pass through the green carriage gates to the left. Do not follow the grass avenue stretching out ahead; instead, strike more or less directly up the slope to the woods, going through the gate just to the right of the prominent knot of trees.

Follow the main path for 50m or so and then branch left on a path heading north out of the body of the trees and along the edge of a conifer plantation, with a clearing to the right. Ignore the two gates and follow the fence back into the trees at Camp Wood. Here, scattered foundations and tumbledown walls mark the edge of an American Forces hospital, built in 1943 and redeployed after the war as a boarding school for Polish refugee girls until it closed in 1954. Follow the path under the canopy

for 100m, then branch left to locate a stile.

Descend through parkland, passing right of the woods. Some 100m into the third field go through the gateway in the wall to the left and continue north towards the cottage. The Stowell Park Estate owns much of the land around here – Stowell Park, the house at its centre, can just be seen up on the brow to the right.

Turn left along the road and then right after 100m to cross the field. Back by the road, brush the corner and bear left through the gate to pick up a path running along the foot of a curving slope and around to gorgeous Yanworth Mill. Turn left, over the roadbridge, and then right before the facing cottage onto a stone track, signed 'Private Road'. Tucked at the foot of a densely wooded slope, with the stream drifting in and out of view to the right, the track makes for an easy, 1.75km stroll back to the Roman Villa road entrance.

To the Slaughters

Distance 7.5km Time 2 hours
Terrain country lanes and tracks and
riverside pastures Map OS Explorer OL45
Access bus services include (801) from
Cheltenham and Moreton-in-Marsh and
(855) from Kemble, Cirencester and
Moreton-in-Marsh to Bourton

If ever there was a reason not to judge a
book by its cover (or a village by its
name), it's in the slightly sinister names
of Upper Slaughter and Lower Slaughter.
This pair of villages, tucked down in the
Eye Valley, are two of the most charming
in the area, celebrated for their mellow,
rustic beauty.

Begin on the High Street in Bourton-on-
the-Water, an attractive if stretched-to-
breaking-point tourist centre in peak
season. Walk west, following the street out
of town to its end at the A429. Cross to the
metal gate opposite (SP Windrush Way),
picking up an enclosed path running along
the bottom edge of a couple of fields. Hop

over the disused railway line and then run
along the foot of a huge, gently sloping
field into a wooded hollow. Turn right at
the fork (SP Gloucestershire Way) and
ascend through a tree-lined corridor out to
a field edge. Join a track and climb north to
the road.

Continue ahead along the roadside for
250m (which is enough – it's a racetrack).
Turn down to the right along an altogether
more peaceful lane (SP Upper/Lower
Slaughter). After 250m bear left along a track
slanting slightly upward. Follow this to its
end, go through the gate, hook back to the
right through another gate and then amble
down through the field to the edge of Upper
Slaughter. Walk down the road ahead to the
small square – a sleepy scene unfolds,
unquestionably pastoral and historic, but
not especially twee. The attractive church of
St Peter (off to the left) is worth a look.

Carry on downwards, past the discreet
entrance to the swanky Lords of the Manor
Hotel (the former Manor House) and

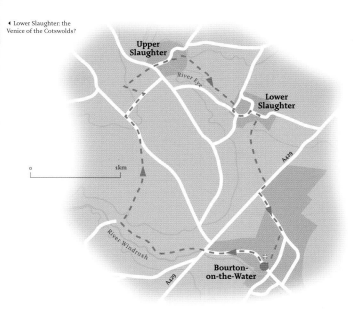

◄ Lower Slaughter: the Venice of the Cotswolds?

around the bend, before branching off to the right along a walled path (SP Warden's Way). Over a tiny footbridge bear right onto a path snaking through a run of lovely meadows alongside the River Eye.

Reaching Lower Slaughter, turn right at Mill Lane, passing the Old Mill craft shop to return to the side of the Eye. Now follow the river through this picturesque village, a glorious balance of water, stone and space that no number of distracted daytrippers can diminish. Join the riverside path by The Slaughters Country Inn, swinging right with the water on a path (SP Heart of England Way) which skirts behind the hotel. Stay on the metalled surface as the way forks and descend towards the roaring A429, the serenity of the villages falling away. Bear right along the roadside pavement for 100m to the pedestrian crossing at the junction with Station Rd.

Head down Station Rd into Bourton. After 400m, just before the entrance to The Cotswold School, bear right along a bridleway slicing between the school and its playing fields, following this to its end at the High St by the neo-classical, dome-topped Church of St Lawrence.

The many ways of Guiting Power

Distance 12km **Time** 3 hours 15
Terrain tight country lanes, woodland
trails, pasture and open escarpment
Map OS Explorer OL45 **Access** limited bus
service (804) from Cheltenham and (819)
(Fridays only) from Stow and Bourton-on-
the Water

**The sweeping views, billowing uplands
and shaded valleys around Guiting Power
make for perfect walking country. Walk
planners have certainly cottoned on; this
half-day excursion looping above the
village coincides with several different
trails – the Windrush Way, Diamond Way
and Gustav Holst Way – with no need to
pack a sleeping bag.**

Set out from the Village Hall (parking) on
Church Rd in Guiting Power. Return to the
village green and bear left along the road.
After 100m, branch right along Castlett St
(SP Warden's Way), following it to its

roughening end and then onto the path
continuing in the same direction. Descend
into a narrow, wooded valley, forking left
just before the stream to rise to open
ground. Pass a farm building and turn
right onto a wide track slicing between
cultivated fields. Cross over a bank and the
minor road upon it and continue along the
track ('unsuitable for motors') with a view
to the left up to a particularly handsome
manor house.

Roll down into the valley, joining a path
left of the cottage which climbs to a tree-
lined trough into Guiting Wood. Levelling
out, pass left of a distinct pine plantation
and across two forestry roads, before
descending to the far side of the wood,
with a minor road seen just beyond the
perimeter. Remaining within the trees,
bear left along a muddy track contouring
just inside the edge of the wood. At the
point where the path moves back up into

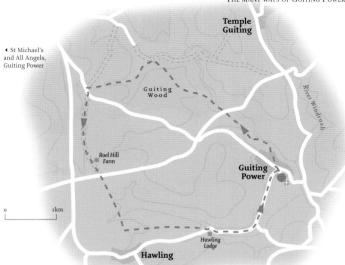

◂ St Michael's
and All Angels,
Guiting Power

Temple
Guiting

Guiting
Wood

River Windrush

Roel Hill
Farm

Guiting
Power

0   1km

Hawling
Lodge

Hawling

the body of the wood, turn sharp right to remain with the edge. Ascend with this much narrower (and less muddy) path for 900m to emerge at a road.

Head left for 100m to the bend, and then branch off onto the bridleway ahead (not the one turning sharp right). Follow the top edge of a cultivated field, with an impressive view opening over the softly-folded landscape. Continue south along the bottom of a blustery pasture – just below the crest of the hill – onto a track leading to Roel Hill Farm. Follow the driveway to the public road and cross to the bridleway opposite (SP Warden's Way).

Now, sticking to the right-hand field edge, descend into a hollow, rise across a spur and then drop into a second cleft,

before climbing back up to level ground. Take the right-hand gate in the wall ahead, onto a muddy, ivy-lined lane. Turn through the first gateway to the left (SP Windrush Way). Head east, joined in the second field by a line of young trees, to pass left of Windrush Farm. Cross a track and then take the gate to the right of the wall ahead, so beginning a direct, steepening descent off the ridge, in the latter stages by way of a track. The views are wonderful. Join the road by the exquisitely manicured environs of Hawling Lodge, swinging left past the farmhouse. It is now a simple case of following the the colourfully named Tally Ho Lane – a narrow but peaceful road – for just over 2km back to its junction with Church Road in Guiting Power.

Belas Knap and Sudeley Castle

**Distance 8.5km Time 2 hours 45
Terrain open pasture and minor roads
Map OS Explorer OL45 Access bus (606)
from Cheltenham and Broadway to
Winchcombe**

**It is the best preserved Neolithic burial
chamber in England, perched on the
eastern edge of Cleeve Hill (the Cotswolds'
highest). Beautifully restored and – at 50m
long and 20m wide – huge, Belas Knap
Long Barrow makes for a fascinating, if
rather eerie, goal on this climb out of the
pretty town of Winchcombe, passing the
grand Sudeley Castle along the way.**

Start by the Plaisterers Arms on Abbey
Terrace in Winchcombe. Head west and
then turn down the tree-lined Vineyard
Street, flanked by rows of low-slung
cottages. Follow the road over the bridge
and out of town, curving right with it by
the entrance to the grounds of Sudeley

Castle. Some 200m on from the bend,
branch right onto a footpath cutting
diagonally across three pastures. In the
fourth field keep to the right-hand edge,
hopping over a stile midway up to follow
the path along the left-hand edge of a
markedly steepening slope. Continue
through a narrow fenced section to pass
the handsome farmhouse at Wadfield and
the rambling, less aesthetically pleasing
outbuildings behind. Join the farm track
and rise to a line of cottages, forking right
of the row to reach Corndean Lane.

Bear right along the lane into trees,
turning up to the left opposite the lay-by
after 500m. A lovely holloway leads
through the wood to a gate at the top.
Swing left along the foot of the field and
then turn up along the far edge to climb to
the hilltop. Keep to the wall on a path
tucked between woods and hedgerow to a
kissing gate, with Belas Knap just beyond.

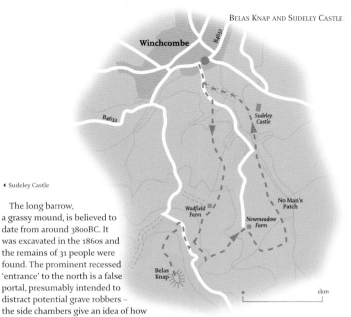

◄ Sudeley Castle

The long barrow, a grassy mound, is believed to date from around 3800BC. It was excavated in the 1860s and the remains of 31 people were found. The prominent recessed 'entrance' to the north is a false portal, presumably intended to distract potential grave robbers – the side chambers give an idea of how the barrow was arranged inside.

Retrace your steps down to Corndean Lane and back to the row of cottages passed earlier. Take the track branching in front of the houses, following this beneath woodland and along the top of the field with a wonderful view across the basin to the folded hills rising behind. Go through gates and turn left to drop down a track to the cluster of buildings at Newmeadow Farm. Bear right along a laid track (SP Restricted Byway), over a dip and on for a further 400m to a sharp right bend.

Leave the track for a path heading north through a pasture. Continue in the same direction through a couple more fields,

with a wood to the right. Where the wood ends, slant diagonally right across two pastures; at the end of the second cross a functional bridge to the right and then go immediately through the gate to the left into the Sudeley Home Parks. Cross the parkland towards the ruined tower of the castle – the rest of the building is largely concealed. Keep within the park to its far end, ignoring the gate out to the adventure playground and parking area. Wander down to the driveway and bear left. Cross the elegant bridge over the small lake and pass the gatehouse out of the grounds. Continue ahead, following Vineyard St back into Winchcombe.

71

A Hailes horseshoe

Distance 7km Time **2 hours**
Terrain **pasture, stone tracks and minor roads** Map **OS Explorer OL45** Access **bus (606) from Cheltenham and Broadway to Winchcombe, 2.5km from start**

Once one of the country's great Cistercian monasteries, Hailes Abbey was smashed after the dissolution in 1539. The romantic ruins of cloister arches and frayed walls remain and, if it is not too busy, it is a fascinating place.

From the abbey walk up the no-through road, branching left along the wooded bridleway by the entrance to Hayles Fruit Farm. Ascend steadily inside the edge of the trees, with regimented rows of fruit trees and plants appearing to the right. Leaving the wood, continue ahead on a grassy track slanting up, past a farm, to the

hamlet of Farmcote. Follow the minor road past the gorgeous, tiny Church of St Faith's and a fine gabled farmhouse.

As the road bends left, split off along a footpath to the right. Walk south across a pair of sloping fields. Into the third, execute a wide arc, first trending left towards the farmhouse and then curving right by the fence. Pick up a green track, passing a ramshackle, corrugated metal shed. Some 100m into the next field, split from the track onto a path cutting left through woodland. Emerging back on open ground a view stretches ahead across the Vale of Evesham.

Follow a wonderful undulating terrace around the upper edge of the field, with a fine view in retrospect to the ribbon of buildings at Farmcote, before descending to move right of the large farm shed at the

◀ Hailes Abbey

edge of Little Farmcote. Go through the farmyard beyond and rise up the left-hand track to the road. Cross straight over and slant up through two horse pastures to a gate on the skyline.

A wonderful and really quite steep descent now unfolds, with the wide, shallow valley stretching ahead. Continue down until an obvious path contouring across the slope presents itself (the Cotswold Way); bear right to follow this northeast through the fields to a track. Swing left down the track to Salter's Lane.

Turn right along this road and then left after 100m along a gravel lane (SP Cotswold Way). A path leads from the lane end across the field beyond, with the abbey just to the right, and back to the start.

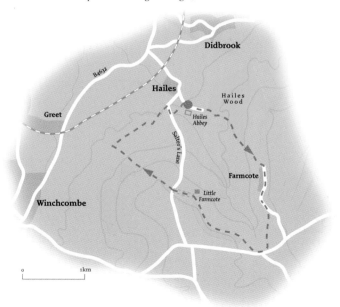

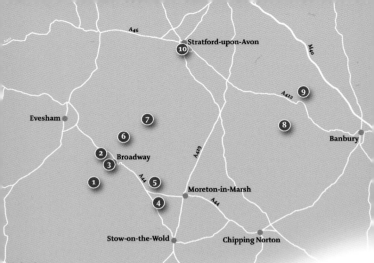

Perhaps the purest expression of what we understand by 'The Cotswolds' is found in the north. Here, the hills make a last glorious stand before sliding down to the lush flatlands of the Vale of Evesham (famed for its fruit and vegetables). Here, the stone is a little darker, more honey in hue than in the south, a last vibrant sparkle before the dull bricked tones of the Midlands. Here, too, is the most beautiful town (Chipping Campden), some of the most beautiful villages (Stanton and Snowshill, for starters), the finest garden (Hidcote), some of the best views (from Dover's Hill and Broadway Tower), two of the finest houses (Sezincote and Compton Wynyates) and, at the furthest reach, Stratford-upon-Avon, a town alive

to the legacy of England's greatest son, William Shakespeare.

Out in the country, there is a gentle pace to life, disrupted only by the tourist trail snaking from honeypot to honeypot. In between, in the places never considered, the area is often at its best – in the beech woods above Mickleton, on the maze of shaded lanes between Stanton and Snowshill, and upon the top of Windmill Hill.

For all its obvious beauty, this is a soothing rather than uplifting landscape with a firm and enduring historical legacy and a gently-spoken sense of 'Englishness'. And out of season, at the margins of the day when the crowds dissipate, even the busiest and most-photographed street finds a serenity.

Edgehill view ▶

The North

Over to Snowshill

Distance 10km **Time** 3 hours 15
Terrain open pastures, lanes, woodland
and minor roads – boots recommended
Map OS Explorer OL45 **Access** bus (606)
from Cheltenham and Broadway calls at
Stanton turning, off the B4632

**Explore the windblown top and shaded
lanes of the ridge rising east of Stanton,
en route to sleepy Snowshill, a golden
hillside village with an extraordinary
manor house at its heart.**

Start from the Village Hall in Stanton.
Follow the road south and bear left along
the High Street to a tiny triangular green,
branching right by the Stott lantern, a
coaching light hanging from a pole. Round
the bend and fork left onto a track out of
the village. After 400m, turn down to the
right, over a stream and into a copse.
Emerging into the open, climb to the right,
guided by Cotswold Way markers, into a
cleft in the hillside (to the right of the
main woods) and up to Shenberrow
Buildings. Pass left of the farmhouse,
through a gate and onto a track.

Follow the track north to a junction with
another; jink left and then right onto a
track to continue north along the top of the
ridge. After 500m, continue ahead along the
Cotswold Way path, ignoring the track to
Laverton Hill Barn. Bypass two further
turnings, this time on the left – one on the
open top and one in descent by woods
– and re-enter fields. Contour
right around the bottom of

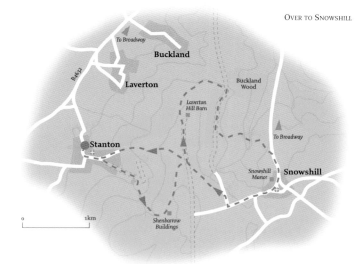

To Broadway

Buckland

B4632

Laverton

Buckland Wood

Laverton Hill Barn

To Broadway

Stanton

Snowshill Manor

Snowshill

0   1km

Shenbarrow Buildings

the field into a second, and then slant right over the crest to meet another lane, this time tucked to the side of lush woodland. Swing right through the gate and return south along the shaded lane.

After 750m, bear off to the left through a metal kissing gate by a copse. Descend the pasture to a wooded dell by the stream in the valley bottom. Head straight up the far side to a gate by a National Trust sign (Snowshill Manor), and then rake right over a hummocky pasture. Cross the entrance to the manor car park and turn right up the road into Snowshill. (If you wish to visit the manor – it is well worth it – turn down the car park driveway.)

Keep right at the junction to pass the side of the manor, the home of English eccentric Charles Paget Wade, who drew together an enormous collection of artisan crafts, historical curios and everyday objects of beauty in his rambling home – 'Let nothing perish,' he said. At the green keep right, pass the Snowshill Arms and church, following the road out of the village and up between wooded banks.

Swing right along the no-through road, pass the house to the right and fork right at the junction. Branch left into the field after 75m and cut diagonally right towards Littleworth Wood (National Trust), aiming to enter the woods midway up. Drift up through the woods along a path to meet a minor road. Bear right along this, soon enough reaching the track junction crossed earlier; continue straight over to weave down the hillside on a lovely and very clear path, reaching Stanton by the Mount Inn. Head back down through sleepy streets to the Village Hall.

◀ The Cotswold vernacular, Snowshill

Broadway's neighbours

Distance 6.5km Time **1 hour 45**
Terrain **old lanes, open meadows and**
pastures Map **OS Explorer OL 454**
Access **bus (606) from Cheltenham and**
Willersey and (21) from Stratford and
Moreton-in-Marsh to Broadway

Loop through a pair of tiny villages
outlying visitor magnet Broadway and
find a quieter, unruffled Cotswolds, a
sedate world of manor houses and old
rectories, oak woods and hillside lanes,
with not a coach party in sight.

Start at the triangular green at the west
end of Broadway High Street. Head south
along Church Street to just beyond the
church and then cross to a lane to the right
(SP Cotswold Way). Follow the lane to its
end and into a meadow, taking the right-
hand path, which leads directly over this
and a second meadow to reach West End

Lane. Cross straight over and take the stile
to the right; follow the metalled surface
the short way to another stile and hop over
into a sloping field. Slant left, up towards
the woods at the top of the field.

Join an undulating path running inside
the bottom edge of lovely Broadway
Coppice. Emerging into the open, contour
around the foot of a steep, curving slope to
reach a stile with the glinting roofs of the
large nursery at Buckland coming into
view. Take the lower path, weaving gently
down to a lane end at the edge of the
village. Wander up the shaded lane, past
some charming cottages (with the Old
Rectory, believed to be one of the oldest in
the country, hidden to the left) to the
'main' road through the village – a wide,
grass-verged avenue. Bear right and then
look for the turning on the left beyond the
phonebox. Keep right of the hedge (SP

◀ Old England glimpsed: the manor and church, Buckland

Public Bridleway) and join a laid path cutting straight to Laverton.

Bear left on the road through the village and along the rough track taking over once the road fizzles out. Ascend for around 150m to a meeting of paths and then bear left to return towards Buckland on a bobbing line across hillside pastures. Pass above the grounds of Buckland Manor, an upscale country house hotel, to a kissing gate and, beyond, a track descending to the village. Hitting the road, turn right, round the bend and continue up to the next corner. Slant left to pass the side of 'The Bothy' and up a short fenced section of path to woods. Ascend between the trees

along the stepped path (not the one to the left), up the grass slope beyond and over the stile to the flat hilltop. Bear northeast into a second field and then move left to follow the wooded field-edge.

At a metal kissing gate the Cotswold Way is rejoined. Turn down into the woods, branching right after 50m onto a path out of the trees and sweeping back down to West End Lane at the point left earlier. Cross over and trace the outward route back into buzzing Broadway.

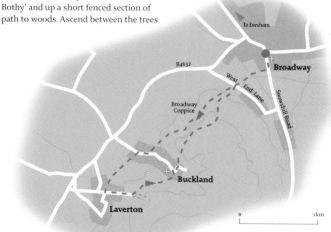

Up to Broadway Tower

Distance **6.5km** Time **1 hour 45**
Terrain **old lanes, open meadows and
pastures** Map **OS Explorer OL45**
Access **bus (606) from Cheltenham and
Willersey and (21) from Stratford and
Moreton-in-Marsh to Broadway**

Broadway Tower is an enduring symbol of
the Cotswolds, a meeting of man and
landscape – doused in history, and topping
the area's second highest hill from which
in clear weather, it is said, 16 counties can
be seen. Although you can motor almost
all the way there, it is much more
enjoyable to do it the (relatively) hard way.

Start at the triangular green at the west
end of Broadway High Street. Walk east up
the High Street, a grand sweep of honey
stone, chestnut trees and grass verges. Bear
right opposite the Horse and Hound pub

onto a path towards an activity park. Pass
right of the impressively equipped
playground and onto a kissing gate at the
field end. A distinct path now runs south
across a run of pea-green meadows to
Snowshill Road.

Bear left along the road to Coneygree
Lane, opposite the picturesque 12th-
century St Eadburgha's Church,
Broadway's only Grade 1 listed building.
Pass through the imposing, ivy-clad stone
gateway and ascend steadily along the
wood-fringed lane. Coming to a T-junction
with another path after almost 1km, bear
right. Go through the gate 75m on and
then rake up the field to beneath a
bungalow. Pick up a track to bear south
towards woods for 200m, then (with
distinctive stone pillars ahead) turn left on
another track. A short way on, by a cluster

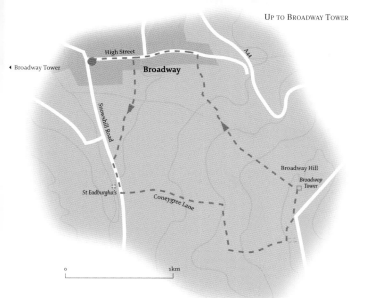

◄ Broadway Tower

High Street

Broadway

A44

Snowshill Road

Broadway Hill

Broadway Tower

St Eadburgha's

Coneygree Lane

0   1km

of cottages and farm buildings, join a metalled lane and continue directly up beside a line of conifers. Once the trees withdraw, go through the next gate to the left and cross the field. Pass the café/shop complex and follow the driveway to just before the road, where a gate leads out to the Tower Deer Park. Head across the undulating top to Broadway Tower.

Commissioned by the Earl of Coventry, and designed by James Wyatt, the faux-fortress was completed in 1799. Like any good folly, it is a flight of imagination serving no particular purpose, other than as a place to see and see out from. Later it proved an inspiration and refuge for William Morris and other members of the

Arts & Crafts Movement. Today, the tower is open to the public with exhibitions on its history. With all that's going on around here, it feels somewhat tamed – it would have been much wilder and lonelier in Morris' day.

Cross the stile to the north (National Trust sign for Clump Farm) and descend left of a dry stone wall towards Broadway, with the Vale of Evesham sliding out to the horizon beyond. Follow the wall down to open fields, slanting northwest with the obvious path (the Cotswold Way) to the village edge. Arriving at the Old High Street, turn left and head back past the High Street's shops and tearooms.

81

Sezincote

Distance 5km **Time** 1 hour 30
Terrain pastures and parkland
Map OS Explorer OL 45 **Access** bus (21/22)
between Stratford-upon-Avon and
Moreton-in-Marsh and various points
in between

**Bourton-on-the-Hill is much less famous
than Bourton-on-the-Water but still very
pretty, though slightly compromised by
the busy road running through its heart.
Starting here, this weaving tour through
verdant pastures and farmland leads to
one of the Cotswolds' most remarkable
houses, the Mogul fantasy of Sezincote.**

Start out from the turning off the A44
down from St Lawrence's Church, a little

side road looping around the church with
some limited roadside parking. From the
red phonebox head 50m up the back road
and then left along a walled green lane (SP
Heart of England Way). The path leads
through a couple of five-bar gates. After the
second, turn sharp left to follow the
fenced-in field edge east through a trio of
lush pastures. Where the fenced section
ends, bear right to follow a corridor
between hedgerows to a small plantation.
Swing left, cross a narrow metalled lane
and resume to the side of a deep green
pasture. Cross a footbridge and skirt round
a small fir copse. Bear south down the left
of the field beyond to a wooded corner.
Turn left over another footbridge and

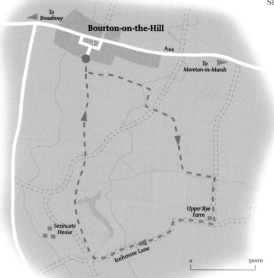

To
Broadway

Bourton-on-the-Hill

A44

To
Moreton-in-Marsh

Upper Rye
Farm

Sezincote
House

Icehouse Lane

0   500m

shadow the hedgerow to an access road.

Bear right along the lane, in the direction of a large agricultural building, to skirt left of the beautiful garden at Upper Rye Farm. By the modern barn go through the gate to the right, joining a metalled lane jinking alongside the field edge and then heading straight up the hill. Just past Keeper's Cottage, turn off through the gate to the right into parkland. Aim for the lone beeches in the middle of the park, an obvious line drifting down through a gateway, with the wood-fringed lake below.

Looking up to the left a fine perspective opens to Sezincote House – the only country house in the area, it can be confidently said, topped by minarets and a copper 'onion' dome, and eulogised by John Betjeman in 'Summoned by Bells'. In 1798, fresh from service with the East India Company, Charles Cockerell set about remodelling his newly inherited home in a peculiar style that is Cotswolds in material and Rajasthan in spirit.

Dip down to a pair of five-bar gates and a sliver of woodland before rising gently through the parkland. Cross the driveway and continue ahead to a pair of kissing gates sandwiching a line of trees. With Bourton now clearly in view ahead, most notably the foursquare Jacobean elegance of Bourton House, traverse a run of pastures towards the village, soon enough meeting up with the lane left at the outset.

◀ Sezincote House

From Blockley to Batsford

Distance 8km **Time** 2 hours 30
Terrain pastures and woodland; plenty of
up and downs **Map** OS Explorer OL45
Access bus (21/22) between Stratford-
upon-Avon and Moreton-in-Marsh and
various points in between

**Criss-cross the lovely ridge southeast of
Blockley to discover Batsford, an estate
village with hardly a stone out of place
and home to a famed arboretum.**

The start is adjacent to the park on Lower
Street, Blockley. Head down Lower Street
towards the edge of the village, turning up
the first road on the left, just after Lower
Brook House (SP Pasture Farm ¾). The stub
of road soon fades into a rough track,
leaving the cloak of trees and rising
through a field to a modern farm building.
Split to the right on a path by the field

edge. Pass through a gate and remain
upwards on a fenced path before swinging
left to contour beneath a line of trees to
another gate, with a fine view reaching
north over the valley. Through this, follow
the curving bottom edge of the field into
another field and then slant right up to a
gate to a road.

Drop downhill by the road to a crossroads,
then turn right to stroll through Batsford –
a perfectly harmonious estate village with
notably ornate and grand stables – around
to St Mary's, an extravagant, spire-topped
Victorian church. Head the short way back to
the bend by Malcolm House and down the
ruler straight, tree-lined avenue. Swing right
at the junction and follow the road for 75m
to a footpath.

A lovely level route now unfolds beside
the perimeter wall of Batsford Park, with

◀ The Stables, Batsford

the house visible in all its glory from midway along. At first glance it appears Jacobean but, in fact, dates from the 1890s when Algernon 'Bertie' Freeman-Mitford replaced an existing Georgian house not to his taste. The house was later the early childhood home of his grandchildren, the 1930s' it-girls, the Mitford Sisters. Today it is emphatically a private house, but the renowned arboretum behind, laid out in the 1860s, is a popular visitor attraction.

After 1km pass through a five-bar gate and continue ahead for a few metres before swinging up along a path at the edge of a pasture (and beside a wood) towards a lodge. Cross the drive to the arboretum and continue straight up the slope. For a time, the route now follows the Monarch's Way, a zigzagging 615-mile walk from Worcester to Shoreham, following the escape route of the future Charles II in 1651. Dive into the woods, remaining with the upward-trending track until it bends sharp left along the base of Century Plantation, then press on ahead in the shadow of a mighty perimeter wall.

Levelling out at the road along the top of the ridge, cross to the lane opposite (SP Heart of England Way). Fork right at the lane end and descend gently by the left-hand field edge with Blockley and its handsome church laid out below. Reaching a shaded lane, bear left across the slope for 100m to a stile on the right, then turn down, resuming the descent through a long, steepening field to Park Farm. Cross the stile to the left of the farm and the driveway, then pass an overgrown fish pond. The path leads to the head of a wooded lane – follow this down to the road, bearing right to climb back into the heart of Blockley.

On Dover's Hill

Distance 7.5km **Time** 2 hours 15
Terrain old lanes, open meadows and
pastures **Map** OS Explorer OL45
Access bus (21/22) between Stratford-
upon-Avon and Moreton-in-Marsh and
various points in between

**The Cotswold Olimpicks is an unusual
and enduring local tradition. Its home is
Dover's Hill, a spur of the scarp rising
high above Chipping Campden which,
in the minds of many, is the
quintessential Cotswolds town.
Combine the two and go for gold!**

If you can drag yourself away from
Chipping Campden's glorious Market
Square, head west along the High Street.
Turn right by St Catherine's Church on to
Hoo Lane – The Hoo being the small hill
rising directly behind the town. Branch left
by the tiny triangular green and, ignoring
various side roads, continue to the head of
Hoo Lane, where it dissolves into a rough
track. Pass a knot of farm buildings and

continue straight up the developing slope
on a path.

Reaching Kingcomb Lane, turn left
alongside the parking area and then cross
to a hedgerow-lined path (SP Cotswold
Way). Out on open ground, bear left to
Dover's Hill trig point. Suddenly the scarp
gives way and you are at the edge, the
ground tumbling down to the Vale of
Evesham to open up a spectacular view.

The hill forms a natural amphitheatre
and it was here that the Cotswolds
Olimpicks were initiated in 1612. In bidding
to host the 2012 Olympic Games, the
British Olympic Association wrote: 'An
Olympic Games held in London in 2012 will
mark a unique anniversary – it will be
exactly 400 years from the moment that
the first stirrings of Britain's Olympic
beginnings can be identified. In 1612, in the
tiny village of Chipping Campden, Robert
Dover opened the first 'Cotswold
Olimpicks', an annual sporting fair that
honoured the ancient Games of Greece.'

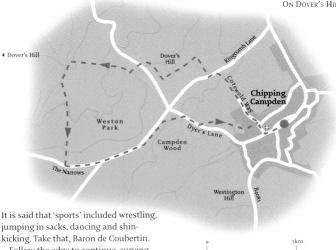

Dover's Hill

Dover's Hill

Kingcomb Lane

Cotswold Way

Chipping Campden

Weston Park

Dyer's Lane

Campden Wood

The Narrows

Westington Hill

Brook

0   1km

It is said that 'sports' included wrestling, jumping in sacks, dancing and shin-kicking. Take that, Baron de Coubertin.

Follow the edge to continue, curving right and turning down the steep slope, away from the car park, at the far end. Descend for 300m, drawing parallel to a minor road, to a kissing gate. Cross the road to a stile opposite and follow a path contouring over a couple of small paddocks, before descending west through a trio of fields and over an access track. Keep right of the houses and aim for the thickets and hedgerow just beyond. Cross a small footbridge over a stream and, keeping to the right of the subsequent field, head up to a second bridge.

Dive into woods and turn up alongside the stream for a steady ascent. Rising out of the trees, stick with a bridleway climbing at the left-hand edge of an open field with an ancient tree-ringed earthwork. Pass left of the grounds of Weston Park (a house) and ascend through

soaring woodland to a minor road, The Narrows. Bear left along this wooded road to a junction, forking left (ahead, more or less). Follow the road along the straight (fast-moving traffic, so take care) to a left-hand bend. By a Cotswold Way sign, dip down to a path running alongside the road. After 400m cut down on a clear path, passing just right of the huge, lone oak, to Dyer's Lane. Turn downhill along the road and through the cluster of houses. A short way on, turn up the bank to the left (SP Public Footpath Chipping Campden). Descend through the field beyond, cutting diagonally down to the edge of town. Walk to the road, cross and follow the path opposite between houses to Hoo Lane. Turn right to return past St Catherine's to the golden High Street.

87

Hidcote and Kiftsgate Gardens

**Distance 6km Time 1 hour 45
Terrain parkland, woodland and some
cultivated fields Map OS Explorer 205
Access bus (21/22) between Stratford-
upon-Avon and Moreton-in-Marsh and
various points in between**

**Two renowned gardens, elegant parkland,
towering Scots Pines and giant beech trees
dot this flora-themed journey up and down
the Cotswold scarp.**

Start from the small parking area at the
lane end just beyond St Lawrence's Church,
Mickleton (turn east off the High Street by
the red phonebox). Walk up the bank to the
left of the gates for Field House (the right-
hand path as indicated by the sign) and
into a field, passing right of the cemetery.
Drop to the right-hand corner after 75m and
go through the kissing gate to a path
through an overgrown hollow. Emerging
into open country, follow the field edge up
the slope of Baker's Hill. Over into the next
field, with a distinctly parkland air, slant

right on the upper path to the road.

Cross straight over to the steps rising
opposite. Curve along the bottom of the
field and then swing right onto a lovely
trail weaving beside giant beech trees
inside the top edge of Baker's Hill Wood –
look for the remarkable collection of
names and initials carved into the trunks,
apparently something of a local tradition.
Out of the trees, follow the top edge of a
cultivated field – the first of a string – to a
roadside hayloft. Bear left on the narrow
road before breaking right after 20m
alongside the right-hand field edge. At the
field end cross a footbridge and then
round the left-hand side of the next field
to a five-bar gate; an avenue beside young
trees now leads up to the road at the edge
of Hidcote Boyce.

Take the road opposite to walk through
the village. At the bend, continue ahead on
the lane past Top Farm. Go through the
five-bar gate at the end, bear left and cut
diagonally across the field to midway

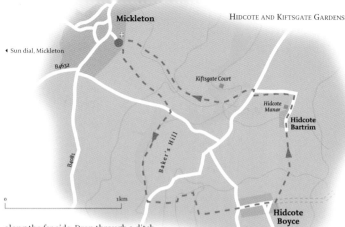

Mickleton

◄ Sun dial, Mickleton

B4632

B4081

Kiftsgate Court

Baker's Hill

Hidcote
Manor

**Hidcote
Bartrim**

**Hidcote
Boyce**

0   1km

along the far side. Drop through a ditch
and continue straight across the next field,
passing the strangely stranded pine in the
middle, to the collection of farm buildings
at the edge of Hidcote Bartrim.

Wander down the lane into this
enchanting hamlet, a near perfect
expression of the Cotswold vernacular. It
may feel a little manicured in places, but
then the National Trust has its grip firmly
on the place. The epicentre of their
influence, Hidcote Manor (to be found soon
enough on the left), is home to one of the
most celebrated of all English gardens,
though ironically it is the work of American-
born Lawrence Johnston. From 1907, he set
out on an ambitious scheme upon the side
of the exposed Cotswold scarp – a garden of
'rooms' of varying degrees of formality, all
within the protection of yews, oaks and
other trees. It is certainly worth a visit.

Continue along the lane to the junction
and bear left. After 20m turn left into the
trees (by the fingerpost) and follow a path

running adjacent to the road through
magnificent woodland. Emerging, carry on
down through parkland to meet a road by
a junction. Bear right and then almost
immediately left through the blue gates
into the grounds of Kiftsgate Court.
Although rather cast into the shade by
Hidcote, Kiftsgate's formal gardens are
open to the public and are of some repute.
A distinct bridleway rolls down the steep
hill, passes through the thin gap left by the
encroaching woods and then slants
slightly left upon the level, cutting across
the park to a gate – in retrospect Kiftsgate,
the house, may be seen up on the bluff.

Leaving the parkland behind, go through
the gate, swing left and follow the edge
of two fields, guided in by the spire of
St Lawrence's ahead. Through another gate
slant right towards the church, picking up
the lane between the churchyard and the
cemetery to return to Mickleton.

The view from Windmill Hill

Distance 3.5km Time 1 hour
Terrain open pasture, lanes and a minor
road Map OS Explorer 206 Access no direct
public transport to start

Stroll past the magnificent house of
Compton Wynyates, one of England's
finest, and discover the tiny stone
windmill atop Windmill Hill.

The first challenge is locating the start
point. Look for the tiny roadside parking
area 250m south of Compton Wynyates on
the minor road between Lower Compton
and Broom Hill, 2km south of Upper
Tysoe. Follow the road northwest down
the wooded slope, passing the drive to
Compton Wynyates, and continue along
the level past Home Farm to a gentle left
bend. Split off to the right, initially along a
tree-lined lane which soon becomes a
fenced track between pastures. As the track
bends left, continue ahead through a

kissing gate and ascend by the right-hand
edge of the field (note the prominent gable
end of the ruined barn just over the fence).
Climb the wooden staircase carved into the
steepening slope to a copse at the crest,
and then swing right through a kissing
gate and wander between the trees to
another kissing gate at the far end.

Now at the edge of open hilltop, bear left
to the windmill, with fine views in all
directions, especially south over the formal
gardens, parkland and irregular roofline of
Compton Wynyates – the house appears to
rest in a bowl, rimmed by low hills.
Believed to be 18th-century, the stubby
little stone windmill no longer turns, but
is a beloved local landmark – a picturesque
reminder of more agrarian days. If you find
yourself here on a windy day you will soon
understand why the builders felt no need
to build the tower higher.

It is now a simple case of retracing the

route back down to the road and on to the gates of Compton Wynyates. This is, unquestionably, one of the great Tudor houses of England, a Mars-red jumble of apparently haphazard gables, chimneys, castellations and mullions. Pevsner found it 'the perfect picture-book house of the Early Tudor decades, the most perfect in England of the specific picturesque, completely irregular mode'. Today, as the signs suggest, its owners protect their privacy and plantings partially obscure the vista down the driveway. It was not always the case: once it was open to the public and for those of a certain generation it will always subsist as the setting for *Candleshoe*, a mid-1970s' Disney film. Indeed, while it has remained in the ownership of the Compton family, the house was in effect abandoned between 1768 and 1835, with windows bricked-up to avoid the 'windows tax.' From here, return to the start.

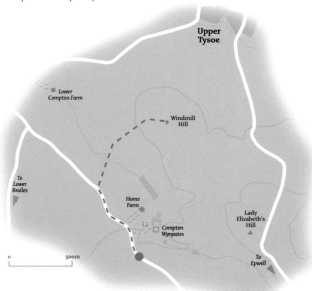

Edgehill battle cry

**Distance 8km Time 2 hours 30
Terrain** lots of woodland, mixed in with
open pasture, cultivated fields and some
road **Map** OS Explorer 206 **Access** bus
(269) between Banbury and Stratford-
upon-Avon

Sun Rising, Edge Hill, Uplands – there is
a theme to the place names in this little
corner on the Oxfordshire/Warwickshire
border – something to do with elevation
and clear views. When, suddenly, you
emerge from the cover of the woods and
stand on the edge of the scarp you see
why – it feels as if half of England
stretches out below. Then throw in the
rich history of a Civil War battle and a
gracious country house.

Set out from the National Trust car park,
Upton House, just off the A422, five miles
northwest of Banbury. From the southern
end, by the coach bays, pick up the
footpath to Home Farm. Round to the
right of the farm buildings (now offices)
and then look left to locate a stile (not the
gate) across the dip. Follow a distinct path
cutting straight across a pair of cultivated
fields to the far corner of the second. Cross
Sugarswell Lane and continue as before,
aiming for the left-hand corner by the
woods. Go through a gate and turn right
along a bridleway at the edge of the trees.
Emerging onto open ground, a wonderful
panorama opens over the plains.

Stick with the edge of the scarp back
into woods and then bear first right on to
a lane by stables before swinging left to
join a concrete track leading down to the
A422. Cross straight over to the woods
opposite. A narrow path slants left, meets
up with a path rising from lower down the
hill and then moves back to follow the top
edge of the woods. This may be one of
those few walks that is at its picturesque
best in the winter months, when no
nettles encroach on the thin ribbon of
path and the foliage falls to reveal the

views over the plain and the battlefield. Either way, it is delightful.

Reaching Edgehill Farm, turn down to the left along the lane and then branch off to the right after 25m, resuming as before. The path briefly runs to the side of fields – press on ahead at the path junction just beyond. Though the battlefield cannot be seen from here, the first major battle of the English Civil War, the Battle of Edgehill, took place at the bottom of the scarp. Some 10,000 Royalists descended the village of Edgehill to engage a similarly-sized Parliamentary Army. Around a thousand men died, but no decisive advantage was gained for either side from this initial engagement.

Coming to a second path junction some 500m on, take the right-hand option of the three available and ascend to Edgehill. Watch out for the Castle Inn (quite literally a castle in miniature) just to the right, surely one of the most distinctive pubs in the country. The octagonal tower was built on the 100th anniversary of the battle to mark the spot where Charles I is said to have raised the standard before commencing the advance down the hill. It has been a pub since 1822.

Cross over to the lane just to the left. A regimented line alongside gardens leads to a road running parallel to the one just crossed. Bear right and then swing left after 50m on to a wide farm track. Follow this to its end and turn right, keeping to the right-hand edge of two fields (past a derelict building) on a gentle descent into a tiny, curving valley. Pick up a green track and rise up the narrowing valley head to Uplands Farm. Keep left of the large agricultural building to the left, joining a track which runs alongside the edge of a pair of fields and down to Quarry Road. Turn right and follow this to its junction with the A422. Cross to the opposite side and bear right, following the wide grass verge past the splendid gateway and long driveway down to the front of Upton House, reaching the car park entrance after 550m.

◀ Edgehill outlook

In search of Shakespeare

Distance 2.5km **Time** 1 hour
Terrain streets, towpath and park
Access Stratford is easily accessible by
public transport

Stratford and Shakespeare are inseparable.
His presence is everywhere, from the place
where he was born, to the place where he
is buried. But this is no cold museum to
past achievement; nowhere is more
dedicated to sustaining and refreshing his
legacy than Stratford, and the streets
around the Royal Shakespeare Theatre
hum with creativity.

There is no better start point than the
beating heart of Shakespeare in Stratford,
the Royal Shakespeare Theatre on
Waterside. Here you find the Royal
Shakespeare Company's flagship
performance space, a 1000-seat auditorium,
gutted and brought bang up-to-date in a
'Transformation' project completed in 2010.
Walk north into Bancroft Gardens (charming
on a sunny afternoon) and towards the
River Avon, cross the elegant curving bridge
over the channel into Bancroft Basin and
head along the path to the Gower Memorial.

A slightly grandiose Victorian confection, it
finds a reflective Shakespeare cast in bronze
atop a sandstone column, flanked by
Hamlet, Lady Macbeth, Falstaff and Henry V
(representing philosophy, tragedy, comedy
and history, respectively).

Follow the basin edge to the road and
cross right over Bridge Foot, taking the
flight of steps ahead down to the canal
towpath. Completed 200 years after
Shakespeare's death, the canal travels
north from the Avon to Birmingham; bear
left in that direction. At Bridge 68 (by
Warwick Rd) cross to the other side of the
canal, rise past Warwick Road Lock and
continue to Bridge 67. Now on road, turn
left over the bridge and pass the pretty
brick terraces of Great William St to its end
at Guild St. Ahead, beyond the railings, is
the rear elevation of the house, now a
museum, where William Shakespeare, the
son of a wool merchant, was born in 1564.
Jink left, cross at the lights and head down
the walkway. Emerging on pedestrianised
Henley St bear right to find the entrance.

Returning down Henley St, pass the fine
timbered library on the left and at the

◀ Themed rowing boats, River Avon

roundabout at the end take the second turning to the right and saunter down the High St, another busy shopping street graced by some ornately-timbered frontages, including the grand sweep of the Shakespeare Hotel, beside which the resolutely classical, Bath stone Town Hall and the red brick Gothic Revival bank building capture four centuries of contrasting architectural styles within a few steps. On the bank building look out for the mosaic of Shakespeare above the front door, and for the wall friezes depicting scenes from the plays.

Press on down Chapel St (leading on from the High St) to the last building on the left before Chapel Lane, Nash's House, a Tudor house presented with period furnishings. Adjacent are the foundations of New Place, where it is believed some of Shakespeare's final plays were written. Just beyond the chapel is the King Edward VI School where, no doubt, the young Bard first revealed his felicity with language.

Reaching the junction with Old Town, bear left towards the leafy grounds of Holy Trinity Church. Midway along, note Hall's Croft to the left, where Shakespeare's daughter, Susanna, and her husband lived, and to the right the pink *Hansel & Gretel* house, surely the city's most distinctive. At the bend turn off into the church grounds and walk up to the building (the oldest in town, dating from 1210). Shakespeare is buried inside, and much of the time the church is open to the public.

Bear left to a gravel terrace overlooking the Avon, and then continue left through an arched gateway into Avon Bank Gardens. The bustle of the town slips away as swans and rowers glide by on the languid river.

A riverside walk now leads all the way back to the Royal Shakespeare Theatre, but do not miss the Courtyard Theatre, the RSC's smaller scale and more 'experimental' venue, and the Dirty Duck pub, a legendary hang-out for off-duty actors, on Southern Lane – which runs adjacent to the gardens. To find these, swing left to the road beyond the Brass Rubbing Centre, located in the classical 'temple'.

95

Index